MODERN ITALIAN SCULPTURE

MODERN ITALIAN SCULPTURE

TEXT BY
ROBERTO SALVINI

73 PLATES IN MONOCHROME
46 PLATES IN COLOR

HARRY N. ABRAMS, INC. · PUBLISHERS · NEW YORK

Library of Congress Catalog Card Number: 59-14795

All rights reserved. No part of the contents of this book

may be reproduced without the written permission of

Harry N. Abrams, Inc., New York

Reproduction rights reserved by S.P.A.D.E.M. Paris, Cosmopress, Geneva

Printed and bound by Stabilimento d'Arti Grafiche Amilcare Pizzi, Milan, Italy

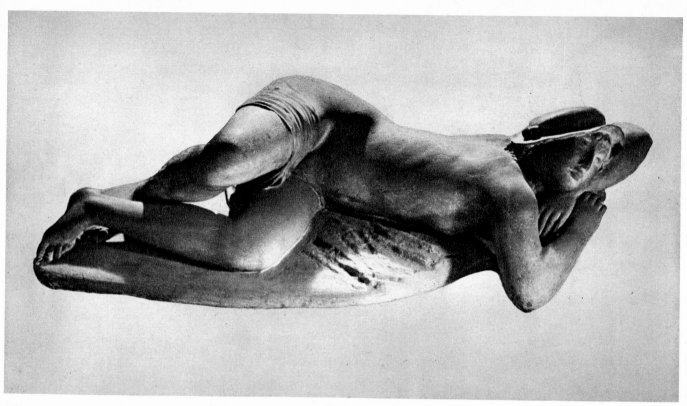

Fig. 1 - Arturo Martini (1889-1947): *Woman in the Sun*, terracotta, 1931.

THE STARTING POINT OF ALL CONTEMPORARY ITALIAN ART IS USUALLY found in Umberto Boccioni, and so this review begins from that point. In other countries, twentieth-century art took its impetus from revolutionary and avant-garde movements that arose at the end of the nineteenth-century and during the last fifty or sixty years its development has been going on in a continually alternating series of explosions, reassessments, revolutions and reactions. The early revolutionary movements that we know under the designation Art Nouveau reached Italy only in weak echoes and so were not able to assume avant-garde importance there. Especially to be noted in this connection were the Vienna Secession and the *stille Liberty* — the latter named, interestingly enough, after the big Liberty's store in London, with its characteristic printed fabrics. Modern Italian art was thus more or less an original movement, and we find no antecedent in Italy for Futurism or for Boccioni, in spite of the bold and inspired work of Medardo   Fig. 2 Rosso Rosso's work was certainly revolutionary, and even extremist, because he thoroughly applied the vision of Impressionism to sculpture (it had always been considered impossible to do so), but he remained tied to Impressionist theory, which was fully nineteenth-century in spirit and incapable of showing the way to further developments.

5

The general theories of Marinetti's Futurism and their more precise application to the figurative arts (largely due to Boccioni), are assumed to be known for the purpose of this critique. The most penetrating analysis of them has probably been made by Maltese, who clearly indicated the close ties existing between Futurism and Bergson's intuitional philosophy; he explains precisely how Boccioni's theory turns Bergson's upside down. For no longer was there to be "transition from motion to rest, and from energy to matter", but on the contrary, transition from the repose of matter towards the energy of movement, towards multiplication and decomposition; the object would explode in a whirlwind of external movement, which embodied energy and spirit, and the spirit creates life.

This is a better explanation of why the new plastic art was defined in the *Technical Manifesto of Futurist Sculpture*, which Boccioni edited in 1912, as "the translation into plaster, bronze, glass, wood and any other material, of the atmospheric planes that bind and intersect things", in order "to bring objects to life, making them capable of being felt, and their prolongation in space systematic and plastic, because no one can doubt that one object ends where another begins, and there is nothing around about our bodies—bottles, cars, houses, trees, streets—that does not cut and intersect them in an arabesque of curves and nets". From this it is clearer than in the preceding *Manifesto of Futurist Painting* (in which the emphasis at first was on "the dynamic sensation made eternal as such"), that the starting point is found in the object, which is static if looked at in isolation, but ready to live and take on life with the most whirlwind-like movement if it is considered in relation to its surroundings. In sculpture, too, the "style of the Movement" had to be attained, and "forcelines" helped towards this end. But in order to do so much it was above all important to overturn the traditional relation between the statue and its surroundings. The statue would no longer be isolated from the environment because of its continuity of line, but there now would be "an absolute and complete abolition of the finished line and of the closed statue. Let us throw open the figure and include the surroundings in it".

These characteristics are all found in Boccioni's sculptural work, which is aimed at the same goal: expressing universal dynamism. But that goal was at the end of a difficult road which was strewn with obstacles, and to get there required hard work on the problem of how object and environment interpenetrate, as set out in the manifesto on sculpture. (In the manifesto on painting this aim is influenced by similar ideas but stands out with a different emphasis). The greater effort required by the theoretical programme is found there too — a series of attempts, in other words, at plastic expression. But Boccioni seems to have attained greater immediate impact and force generally with pictorial expression, in spite of the fact that, when he attempted sculpture, he was able to derive benefit from the theories of Cubism, of which he became aware at a rather advanced stage of his painting career. One may well ask whether valid artistic features are not to be found more readily in his paintings than in his sculptures. Fundamentally, Boccioni's personality as a painter had already been clearly expressed in his divisionist experiments, and some of these paintings — such as the *Portrait of the Sculptor Brocchi* — already have a full and explosive luminosity unreservedly expressing joyous abandonment to, and a sharing in, the universal breath of life. Even though of later sought more emphatic forms in the style of Munch and early Expressionism, here he was looking only for a more vigorous and incisive language. Indeed he was able to produce his first Futurist painting — *La Città Sale* (*The City Ascends*) — and the whole series of rapid preparatory sketches and studies, without giving up his own divisionist technique. Calvesi's literary investigations have recently been able to fix the dates and manner of Boccioni's first contacts with Cubism. In 1911 they were indirect but already fruitful, as we see from his critical articles published in the summer of that year. In the following November he was in Paris and made direct but rather hasty contact; in February, 1912, he returned there and was able to deepen and clarify these contacts. Thus his approach to Cubism, and to Picasso in particular, has a story of its own. He was never submissive, but always very watchful, alert and polemical — even too much so.

The lasting result of this experience was that the original nucleus of his painting was enriched with new themes and new flexibility of expression. The very essence of his art had, however, already matured in the light of different, though perhaps less stimulating, experiences. It was otherwise with his sculpture, though at first Boccioni wished to do in sculpture what, a year before, he had begun to do in painting — both in his own work and together with a close group of colleagues. (In the manifesto there is a strong reminder of the recent achievements of Futurist painting.) His second journey to Paris was on the occasion of the Exhibition of Futurist Painting held there in February, 1912. The manifesto bears the date of April of that year, and there are reasons for believing that Boccioni made his first attempts at sculpture about the time this was drawn up. One of these sculptures is called *Empty and Full Abstracts of a Head*, and shows that his starting point was in Cubism, which he had studied in some heads by Picasso. Boccioni's work is certainly of the greatest interest, especially if we look at it bearing in mind the principles laid down by the manifesto and keeping an eye on some of Picasso's above quoted sculptures. Then it is abundantly clear how the moderate Cubist analytical technique of Picasso's manner, moving away from form, gave Boccioni the technical means and vocabulary to put into practice those principles of the manifesto that were largely derived from the intellectual basis of the Futurist movement. The idea of opening out the form of the object so

PL. III

7

Fig. 2 - Medardo Rosso (1858-1928): *Motherhood*, bronze.

as to receive its environment was, at this stage, limited to the surrounding atmosphere; it was expressed in concrete terms, and avoided any surface pictoriality in the empty spaces (for that would have taken it back to Impressionism in the manner of Medardo Rosso). At the same time the "static muscular line was transformed into the dynamic forceline" since "the straight line will now predominate, for it alone corresponds to the inner simplicity of the synthesis which we set up in opposition to the baroque exteriority of analysis". This is why some profiles rise up and are incisively stretched out, as in Picasso, while elsewhere there is a predilection for straight lines, the "naked and fundamental severity of which" (the manifesto says) "shall be the symbol of the steely severity of the lines of modern machinery." This preoccupation with absorbing the surroundings into the empty spaces by creating a division between the filled and empty areas is so regular and so lacking in imagination that the result — though certainly not the intention of the

8

artist — is substantially static, and breaks up the suggestion of dynamism, expression-istically portrayed and derived from Picasso.

We will not deal with the well-known creations from miscellaneous materials, for instance, the *Fusion of a Head and Window; Head, House, Light,* in which iron rings, window blinds and fragments of glass and tufts of hair are embedded in the plaster, and which were executed as strict examples of other concepts of the manifesto. We should notice the involuntary metaphysical characteristics of *Development of a Bottle in Space,*   Pl. II probably one of Boccioni's earliest sculptures, and a work in which a bottle with its side torn out develops from the circular movement and expansion of the forms of its central nucleus, and is itself interpenetrated by space. This work was executed in ac-cordance with the whole gamut of manifesto principles and with such didactic conscien-tiousness and craftsmanlike honesty that the sculpture almost comes to look like some precious ornament—a paperweight, or an inkwell of the latest design. These early Boccioni sculptures have thus a wholly intellectual and doctrinaire bias, and I find it difficult to agree that his programmatic work receives original artistic intuition from them. This does not deprive the works of considerable artistic importance, since in their own time they were certainly the most advanced and boldest efforts yet made in that process of tearing away sculpture from its monumental traditions, so characteristic now of much contemporary sculpture; and they also display equal ingenuity in putting forward new themes, subjects and forms. On the other hand, similar studies in the interpenetration of object and environment develop into a search for regularity, volumetric equilibrium and firmly executed perspective. Some drawings show this, like the one called *Table, Bottle, Houses.* These qualities do not fit in well with Boccioni's declared aim of dynamism, but they already reveal a tendency towards monumental calm that will bring him in his last paintings unexpectedly close to Cézanne.

Very soon, in 1912, Boccioni moved some distance away from the manifesto's for-mulae, since he had already discovered that the forceline based on the straight line was substantially static. So he began a search for clearer dynamism, and introduced and multiplied ellipses, developing his compositions with convex planes and helicoid rhythms. Thus the *Portrait of his Mother* was entitled *Antigrazioso* (anti-graceful) in accordance   Pl. IV once more with one of the aesthetic postulates of the manifesto. It doubtless succeeds in producing a fairly coherent interplay of surfaces, which seem to breathe, working to-gether to share in the life of the body and of space. But a physical resemblance persists — we can compare it with one of his realistic drawings of his mother's face — and in the end it introduces associations of ideas that disturb the effect. There is also a baroque

9

emphasis, the danger of which Boccioni himself had warned against. In the manifesto he had rejected such a possible accusation against Futurism. This baroque emphasis is

Pl. I, V notable also in the three statues: *Synthesis of Human Dynamism, Muscles in Rapid Action,* and *Spiral Expansion of Muscles in Movement,* which nevertheless are of the greatest importance when considered as preparatory studies for the *Unique Forms in the Continuity of Space,* which is his best known and only fully successful sculpture.

Fig. 3 If we look at a series of drawings, one of which is reproduced here, connected with his studies in this kind of composition, we may guess how the artist was ill at ease when he tried to translate into sculptural terms the kind of figure that had flashed into his mind with the purity and rapidity of lightning but took shape more easily in the language of drawing and painting. But this unsatisfying labour was fruitful, for in less than a year

Pl. VI after the first of these attempts, the superb figure of the *Unique Forms in the Continuity of Space* was born of his imagination and settled into the luminous forms of its bronze. His undisciplined, contradictory, and exuberant shapes have been purified into the extremely fine formal coherence of the elastic and continuous rhythm of spiral lines, and luminous and continuous surfaces. Now for the first time each form really belongs to space as well as to the object, and for the first time the figure embodies the idea of whirlwind and continual motion. Boccioni's joyful dedication to movement as the essence of life explodes into a state of gay optimism.

This, be it noted, is Boccioni's last piece of sculpture, and the fact that he did not halt his rapid succession of anxious sculptural experiments until he had finally reached a positive artistic result says much for the clarity of his critical sense.

The result was positive, but exceptional. Boccioni was above all a painter, and to painting he gave the last years of his life, cut off so prematurely by the war (he died August 16, 1916.) During these last years he began researches in another direction, which foreseeably would have soon led him to abandon his Futurist artistic theory.

Roberto Melli, who also had a painter's temperament, occupies a notable position alongside Boccioni in this experimental phase of modern Italian sculpture, though he did not take part in the Futurist movement. His few works of sculpture belong to the preparatory period of his art, both for obvious chronological reasons and because the artist finally found his vocation as a painter while engaged in this laborious search for a plastic language. He took upon himself the task of solidifying Medardo Rosso's Impressionism, and obeyed the demands of his own sensibility rather than the requirements of programmes and theories. At first, as in the *Portrait of a Child* in wax (1906), he forced the movement of the forms into a discipline derived from ingenuous and summary

Fig. 4, 5 archaism. Later, as in the matured group of sculptures of about 1913 — two are

10

Fig. 3 - Umberto Boccioni (1882-1916): *Muscular Dynamism*, charcoal, 1912-13.

reproduced here — a less forced plastic regularity is joined by an alternating but very strict interplay of full and empty spaces, giving a highly tonal value to the work. Certain stylistic characteristics, which derive from the technical idiom of Cubist and Futurist analysis, take on profoundly different meaning, and the luminous fluidity of his surfaces forms an authentic process of solidifying Impressionism. The image thus arises from an objective appraisal of the natural aspect of the object in its vital relation with atmosphere and light, which is immediately projected as if on to a distant screen, and thus the volume is fixed as a motionless concretion of light. Melli's ideas now became perfected productions, arising from his sense of wonder at a dazzling reality in light; they also made full use of the extreme limits of the expressive possibilities of sculptural language. In its urge to take on another shape, to enrich itself still more with even subtler nuances, his art demanded to be transposed into the language of painting, and thus Melli found his true vocation. It was as a painter and no longer as a sculptor that he equipped himself to make his own fundamental contribution to the Plastic Values movement. Nevertheless it is true that those artistic ideas that would find their most perfect expression in his painting were first expressed in these few bronzes, which are among the most authentic works to be found in the first period of modern Italian sculpture.

PL. VII, VIII For Modigliani, sculpturing was also an exceptional activity. He was led to make experiments under Brancusi's influence (he shared his studio) at the very time when artistic Paris was full of enthusiasm for Negro carving. He neglected the easier course of modelling and like Brancusi took the harsher one of working with chisel on stone. Obviously Brancusi's ovoid forms represented a welcome stylistic inspiration: Modigliani's few sculptures are stamped with an undeniable mark of originality. An immediate benefit derived from Negro art was a general air of archaism, serving to add emphasis to a sharp deviation from the canons of beauty found in ancient Greek sculpture — which Modigliani presumably had also studied attentively. On the other hand, Brancusi's egg shapes are rendered with the preciousness that was the very basis of all Modigliani's artistic formation. Modigliani's work is an exercise in extreme stylization, and undoubtedly was influenced by a "decadent" culture and was an act of homage to the fashion for the exotic which was revived at that time by the *Fauves* and Expressionists. This is the origin of these strange figures, in which the smile of archaic Greece fuses with the sensuous mystery of the idols of Polynesia.

Such, then, is the sculpture of the first Italian avant-garde. Its theoretical labours were followed by artists, movements and theories of varying degrees of intelligence and sensibility, all orientated towards the return to order and tradition. During the twenties these tendencies culminated in the *Novecento* movement, which was officially favoured

Fig. 4 - Roberto Melli (1885-1958): *Portrait of the Critic V. Costantini*, stone, 1913.

Fig. 5 - Roberto Melli: *Woman in a Black Hat*, bronze, 1913.

by the Fascist regime, and had complex and contradictory aspects. It united several modern tendencies deriving from Cézanne, and in this way it once more took up the task of consolidating Impressionism, which had been the basis of all innovating movements at the beginning of the century. Its tendencies were more strictly traditional and capable of fitting in with the ideological climate of the time. In this atmosphere favoured by a craftsman's instinct and self-taught technique, the personality of the official sculptor of the time, Francesco Messina, was developed, and he is still fully active today. Basically he represents the return to, and continuation into, the modern period of the late nineteenth-century traditions of Verismo. From Verismo he takes his firm plastic construction, his conscientious realism and stylistic versatility; in brief, his general ability to introduce notes now and then from this or that language of a past period — all in a uniform atmosphere of neo-Renaissance. Messina won his first laurels in the

Pl. XVII field of portraiture. His likenesses are perfect, his poses monumental and notable for psychological penetration of the subject. But he has given and still gives proof of equal ability in full-length sculpture, ranging from his series of statues celebrating athletes

Pl. XVIII to his other series of female nudes. To the latter, especially in his more recent works, he has succeeded in giving pictorial sensitivity by introducing elements of the purest naturalism. His work is always and above all that of a virtuoso. In some of his recent male nudes, like those in the Cini collection, he shows signs of wishing to absorb something of the artistic qualities of the mythical, the archaic and the fragmentary.

Arturo Martini also belonged to the *Novecento* for a short period, but his participation had an entirely different significance. Maltese declares that in the ranks of the *Novecento* two fundamental tendencies may be discerned "in every metaphysical tone of every landscape, every still life and every example of its dominating archaism: an *art de régime* and an *art d'évasion*". If so, then Martini's place was with the *art d'évasion*. He escapes from an unpleasant and suffocating reality, but he is also deeply interested in the search for form, which he understood as the working out of a language capable of expressing a new concept of art. We find neither clear and unequivocal stylistic formation nor clear development in Martini. Late nineteenth-century Verismo, Art Nouveau, Hildebrandt's classicism, "Plastic Values", and *Novecento*, in the deep meaning given it by Carrà, are some of the principal sources of Martini's language. He matured slowly. Even after he had found his style—about 1926—there is surprising variation in his work, because he saw his figures as if reflected in the continually changing mirror of ancient sculpture: Hittite, Greek archaic, Roman portraiture, Etruscan realism. The reason is not poverty of imagination nor eclecticism, but that he has to cope with the diversity of his themes — one of his ambitions is to overcome even the most difficult problems — and because

14

of the diversity of his materials — another of his ambitions is to force the most disparate materials to his own will for expression. He seeks aid from various sources, all of which are necessary for him, and he immerses his figures in a mythological atmosphere. He sees nature and humanity in the mirror of myth — never a conventional or official myth, but one with an air of legend and popular fable, or one which is a means for him of sinking voluptuously into the vital breath of nature. In his first period of great creative fertility — a little less than ten years centred around 1930 — his figures (as in the *Motherhood* group) are stylized and have simplified surfaces. The observer feels an extraordinarily Pl. X immediate appeal, and becomes aware of their character as legendary images called forth from vague distances in time, in order to embody a real human emotion. The babies crawling on their mother's body in *Motherhood* are not just facile and sentimentally descriptive; the emotion is *completely* expressed in formal language through the group's superior unity, which arises from the pulsating softness of relief and modelling. A vivid sense of atmosphere is created, both by the porousness of the surfaces and by the skilful, though not immediately apparent, arrangement of the figure in space. This atmosphere deepens the vital human truth of the composition. In the *Resting Athlete* of 1930, both the lack of arms and the general stance — vaguely in the style of Lysippus — help to evoke an atmosphere of myth about the figure. But this mythical atmosphere is not imprisoned by these archaic forms in its own world, for it plummets with all its human force into our present reality. The delicate sensibility of the modelling and free placing in space (once more, not immediately apparent, but highly natural) give stylistic value to the suggestion of portraiture conveyed by the lines of the face, the half-open mouth and the gazing eyes. The effort that the athlete has just made and the distance he has covered are suggested by the intensity of the portrayed emotion. This capacity to evoke a sense of space about the figures, a space where the feelings of the subject may expand and reverberate, creates effects of extraordinary depth in certain bas-reliefs of this period, such as the famous *Dream* and the *Claire de Lune*. In the latter, the surroundings are Pl. IX represented with extreme simplicity and great evocative power. The motif of two women leaning on a balcony is immediately and clearly rendered. We become aware that the balustrade is made of six heavy time-worn Doric columns, that the women are wearing long gowns resembling Greek tunics, that the surfaces of the figures share the worn aspect of the pillars, and that this erosion is accompanied by extremely tender modelling, and merges with the forms bathed in the soft light from the moon. The suffused look of the two faces is due to the presence of the moon. Thus the mixture of realistic and descriptive devices is transfigured in an evocative atmosphere, the theme is projected into timeless antiquity, and we recognize a state of wonder and dreaming sweetness.

Analogous effects and a similar lyric tone are expressed in statues of this same period, such as the *Pisana*, inspired by the heroine of Nievo's novel, and the *Woman in*

Fig. 1 *the Sun.* There are already signs of freer abandon to the happiness of nature, which will be the dominant motive of many works after 1940. These bold works show Martini's gifts of inexhaustible formal invention for, never satisfied, he is always in passionate conflict with the material and with the very technique of sculpture, which he has disconsolately described as "a dead language" — a dead language because during its long history it seems to have worn out all possible means of expression. The slavery imposed by the material sets an impassable limit, for: "Sculpture (unlike music, painting, etc.) was not and can never be *merely* sculpture, because its creative means are not volume and form, but clay."

Indeed, Martini's latest works give the feeling that they have reached the extreme limits of the expressive possibilities of sculpture and are now impelled by an undisciplined and unrestrained imagination — which is nevertheless still capable from time to time of

Pl. XI creating figures of absolute artistic worth. An example is the *Woman Swimming Underwater,* where the movements of the swimming body are rendered without the least technical description, and with such unifying force that the figure appears to be living entirely in

Pl. XIII trustful and voluptuous abandonment to the water. And though his *Livy* does not succeed in overcoming the limits of official and traditional art, other works, like the *Resting Athlete*

Pl. XV of 1941 and *The Partisan Masaccio* (portrayed as the mythical Palinurus) of 1946, do show signs of artistic value which have not been fully worked out, but which are evident in the tension between the still visible classical source and the departure from ancient proportional and spatial principles in favour of impassioned striving towards the freedom of space and the freshness of the air. This striving is the most vivid element in the group

Pl. XII of *Daedalus and Icarus,* where, however, the attempt to soften the two figures by means reminiscent of the *Rondanini Pietà* does not seem to have been very successful.

But amongst his successes in recent years we may perhaps count those figures of

Fig. 6 bulls and cows, in which deep hollows open in the volume itself, and protuberances arise from the surfaces and are connected with each other so as to accentuate the play of light and shade, voluptuously immersing the form into the throbbing, immense life of nature.

Arturo Martini's "irregular" temperament and his volcanic personality were enough to stop him from forming a school of his own. But in a more general sense, his example had great value and certainly contributed to keeping younger sculptors away from the easy conformity of *art de régime.* His work contributed more than any other previous attempt of avant-garde iconoclasm to renewing Italian sculpture and leading its taste back to modernity.

Fig. 6 - Arturo Martini: *Cow*, bronze, 1940.

But young artists growing up in the art of the 1930's would have had great difficulty in advancing along his road, and so we find that one of the greatest of living sculptors, Giacomo Manzù, on his own account went back to work through the historical experience of Tuscan Renaissance sculpture right up to Medardo Rosso; he modelled himself on Rosso in order to discover the extreme point of impressionistic dissolution of form, and to seek in it the beginning of a way towards its modern reconstruction. Manzù's *Susanna* of 1936 and the *Portrait of Signora Vitali* of 1939 come to mind; they follow a long series of heads more directly connected, in theme at least, with Rosso's work. The brilliantly flashing, instantaneous impact of Rosso's figures is recreated in them with pictorial intensity and much greater deliberation. Delicately vibrating planes of light and slowly rounded forms seem to cause a portion of space to curve with them and create a kind of halo about the figure. The expression is sad and absorbed and has an atmosphere of tenderly affectionate intimacy with the real and the human. Such a feeling of affectionate and sensuously intimate contemplation takes on greater attachment and produces more monumental results in his more recent periods, which are concentrated

17

on two themes, apparently opposed to each other but in reality complementary: the *Cardinals* and *Dancers*. The *Seated Cardinal*, in bronze, of 1948 is a first example of a new phase. The sculptural mass has a firm and tranquil unity of its own, because the figure has been quietly modelled into a large bell-like form, which gives it a kind of absorbed isolation. The broadly spread surfaces and the slow rhythm of the folds of the delicate modelling immerse the sculptural material in tranquil light, which the surfaces absorb and reflect, giving a tonal effect that could even remind us of the *Sacraments* of Giuseppe Maria Crespi. Thus, space is enclosed about the figure, claustral shadows hover over the image of the prelate, and we experience warm sympathy for the good old bishop who has dozed off during his evening meditation.

Pl. XXIII, XXIV   Later, as in other *Cardinals* and *Little Cardinals*, a sense of the hieratic isolation of the figures is suggested by further simplification of the arrangement, smoother capes, and surfaces resembling cloth and imbued with light. There has been talk of religious profundity, even of mysticism, in Manzù. The feeling of these works is, however, one of ingenuous wonder born of affectionate observation; I do not believe that mystic elevation is present in them, but that the artist is sensuously interested in the mystery of the holy man and shares in it. These works correspond perfectly with the contem-
Pl. XIX   porary series of female nudes, in which the body surfaces are so sensitive to light that they take on intense tonal value, while the body itself is closed in a locked construction, a kind of idealized dance step, and the artist feels silent wonder and reverent affection before mysterious and sensuous, happy, vital nudes. Thus understood, the two basic themes of Manzù's recent work can be seen as opposite poles of the field of the artist's
Pl. XX   intuitive sympathy. Another proof is to be found perhaps in the *Girl on a Chair* and
Pl. XXI   in the *Bust of Inge*, where winning sensuousness and absorbed contemplation, secret vitality and hieratic firmness meet together in a superior unity.

Attempts have been made to interpret the art of the two greatest and now " classic " living sculptors, Manzù and Marino Marini, by beginning from their rebellion against the *Novecento* with its acceptance of official art and *art de régime*. A sorrowful protest against violence and war has been seen in the reliefs of the *Crucifixion* and *Deposi-tions* executed by Manzù between 1938 and 1942 and a satire on Mussolini in Marini's early *Horsemen*. Likewise an attempt has been made to apply the role of " Catholic opposition " to Manzù, and that of "lay opposition" to Marini. Such motives could have had some value and some part in their choice of subjects and of some of their attitudes, but we do not agree either with such political interpretations of their art nor with those who want to see Manzù, almost in spite of himself, as representing a return to classicism and reproach Marini for coldness and the detachment of an artist dedicated to merely formal problems.

18

Fig. 7 - Giacomo Manzù (1908): *Drawing*.

There are far different things in the work of these artists. I have referred already to the feeling of Manzù's work, but it is certain that Marini's archaism and search for form are aimed first of all at catching the whole of the critic's attention. As soon as we realize that his archaism is pre-classical — Mediterranean and Etruscan — we can understand his deeper motives and intentions. The dominating themes of his work are portraits with roughened and eroded surfaces, as if just fished out of an undersea cavern or from the bottom of an archaeological excavation: female nudes in rich variations on the theme of turgid carnal plenitude, horsemen and horses, pulsating, replete, swollen, or very thin, motionless on their four outspread hoofs, or in flight, caught in the middle of the most unlikely leaps. Common to them all is the characteristically rough and fragmentary execution, which nevertheless has powerful architectonic stability. Such plastic ideas may be oversimplified, but they do avoid the ultimate perfection and static fullness of geometry. Marini's figures all live in an atmosphere of very ancient, pre-classical, if not anti-classical forms, which possess a clarity and authority of expression that brings them close to classical productions. Marini tried his hand at painting for a long time before taking up sculpture and was trained at the school of Domenico Trentacoste, the inheritor of nineteenth-century Verismo. I would say that he spent his long and promising period

Pl. XXVI of formation — from about 1930 until after 1940 — in patient and impassioned search for formal expression, inspired by a general feeling for the primitive spirit. When they show through his severe preoccupation with formal thought, the lyrical qualities of his art also spring from the evocative capacity of those same images, resulting in more and more precise expression of his deep originality; and today in the light of his mature productions he deserves to be judged very differently. It is now clear that Marini is not merely making a display of formal inventiveness, but is presenting us with blocks of material that are still in the process of taking shape. It has been said that Marini is not just a rough-hewing sculptor but a typical modeller, for he makes no effort to hide the point from which he began with the shapeless matter, and attributes a mysterious shaping power to the material itself. When the process of taking on shape reaches a certain point of maturity, it is unexpectedly baulked by the opposing pressure of surrounding space. That shows — and it could be confirmed by a closer analysis — that the artist's inspiration derives from an ever renewed and always provisional dialectical synthesis of two opposite motifs; on the one hand reverent and wondering astonishment at the primordial striving of matter towards light and the emotion felt in the presence of primitive, absolute sensuality; on the other hand, equal admiration at the presence of the opposing disciplinary force, the pressure exerted by space, which intervenes to arrest the instinctive growth of matter, and then firmly forms it into the design. Matter as an obscure power of vital expansion and space as a

Fig. 8 - Marino Marini (1901): *Horseman*, drawing, 1952.

geometric area of the spirit, understood as rule and order, are the two opposed principles, and from their collision form is born. This presupposes a vision of life as conflict, or dramatic tension, between disordered but creative matter and the discipline of spirit — (not too Aristotelian an interpretation, because the stress must be placed on the clash of the two forces rather than on their mutual comprehension, and the lyric centre of this vision is in fact expressed by a rich scale of substantially dramatic overtones). Also, where that mysterious vital energy of matter seems to succeed in expanding freely into full, swelling forms, the external pressure remains none the less evident, and at times painfully so, in the erosion of the surfaces which, arching and bending, offer themselves to the dazzling

Pl. XXV   light. This is characteristic of his earlier works, from his first maturity of vision, practically from 1940-45 onwards (nothing before that date quite succeeds in freeing itself from the bonds of highly intelligent experimentation with form and the search for a point of

Pl. XXVII, XXX   view). In the last fifteen years, the vital impulse has continued to acquire greater and greater tension, and the signs of pressure from space are marked more and more harshly on the material. This can be verified by examining at random only one of the three series : portraits, nudes, horsemen. The dramatic note becomes stronger and stronger until in the last group the horses rear up in spasmodic tension, the riders leap from their saddles in anguish.

To undervalue Marini's archaic inspiration and that taste for form and the primordial image that are the constant and characteristic concomitants of his work would be equivalent to asserting that his long apprenticeship with Egyptian and Etruscan sculpture, his studies of the more anti-classical aspects of Roman portraiture and statuary, and his later preoccupation with themes culled from the Aegean and even from China had all been useless; it would entail rejecting the most obvious aspects of his language and banishing one of the central themes of his artistic conceptions to the borders of criticism as mere inexplicable residue and aesthetic ballast. We must not disregard the mythological tone in Marini's work, because his archaism and myth are not sentimental escape into the world of fable, not even allegorical or symbolic renderings of moral truths. The archaic basis of his language and the atmosphere of primordial myth deriving directly from it are a poetical way of rising at one leap through the whole course of history, and of carrying that fascinating struggle, in which the discipline and clarity of the spirit is opposed by the obscure wildness of matter, back to the primordial things, the very origins of life — beyond the threshold of time as it were — thence to bring forth the fantastic images of a new cosmogony.

It has been asserted that Marini's art is to be valued (or deprecated, according to one's views or the aesthetic theory one begins with) because of what it brings to the problem

22

of form abstractly (and therefore inartistically) considered and not, like every true art, because of its happy fidelity both to form and to human content. But it is my conviction that this rather widely held view about him will collapse in the light of the views here advanced, though my own interpretive sketch may need deepening, greater precision, or even correcting.

We find a different concept of myth in the work of Mascherini. He too grew up in the atmosphere of the *Novecento* but by temperament and honesty kept away from *art de régime*. At first he wavered between escape into archaism and dedication to faintly sensuous naturalism in the manner of Maillol, and I would say that the works of his most recent and mature period, from 1950 onwards, are characterized by a synthesis or fusion of these two attitudes. Indeed his naturalistic impulse, notable for its serene, frank, but not unseemly sensuousness (from the *Summer* of 1930 up to *Woman by the River* of 1943), has become more and more refined through additions to his cultural knowledge, continued to be acquired from a series of researches into archaic sources (the culture of the Dipylon, to that of Tanagra and elsewhere), and through a spirit of pastoral lyricism and reawakened myth.

A few years ago, in a commentary on his *Faun with a Pipe* (1954), I was able to point out a parallel with Giambologna. I wanted to show how lyricism can arise even from a mannerist spirit. For his more recent *Faun* (1958) I could repeat now, word for word, what I wrote then about the relation between the originally hedonistic theme and its strictly formal working out in this triangular, very well defined composition — except that now there is stronger emphasis on the immediate in the highly sharpened silhouette. The evocative value of the serene and playful atmosphere of sylvan myth remains fundamentally as before. A good recent example of the spontaneity with which the sculptor's fresh and naturalistic sensibility is expressed through the figures of Greek myth, is to be found in the evocative figure of the centaur in the *Corrida*. But Mascherini's very latest successful variations on his lyric theme are perhaps the bronze *Sappho* of 1958 and the *Chimera* of 1960. In the former, the shape has been more softly modelled; it has fuller roundness, the artist has thought about it longer, and he has sought after a more tender vision. In the *Chimera* the form unexpectedly expands from a sharp stem into mysterious immobility, and the dynamic and gushing vitality of the shapes is even coloured by surrealist suggestion. Thus in his more inspired moments Mascherini resolves the discord between highly audacious naturalism and over-refined stylization. This discord is manneristic in the sense of sixteenth-century Mannerism.

Emilio Greco has no need to turn to the myths of the past in order to emphasize the Hellenising flavour of his taste; for it is natural to him, and he is content to render the

Pl. XXXI

Pl. XXXIII
Pl. XXXII

Pl. XXXIV

23

modern and gallicizing theme of the *Bather* in the luminous atmosphere of the Greek spirit. The theme of the female nude preponderates in his work, and we find a primitive impulse of happy abandonment to nature in it, felt in pagan fashion as outright, simple, innocent and sensuous. Perhaps it is in this serenely pagan attitude, nourished on a literary but none the less spontaneous awareness of his native, happy Hellenic past (for he was born and reared on the east coast of Sicily), that we can discover the deep reason for Greco's archaism: he does not escape into aesthetic formalism, but looks for historical justification for his original instinct that is seeking expression. The mental and imaginative road that has brought this artist to his most lyrical utterances has consisted in progressively refining and ennobling those original impulses of " imaginative sensuousness " (in Ragghianti's words). He has a moderate attitude towards the ideal forms born in his imagination during his study of late archaic Greek art: and he moves from the harmonious modelled solidity of Attic Korai towards Ionic over-refinement, such as is found in the *Birth of Venus* and the nude girl flautist of the *Ludovisi Throne*. Thus his art oscillates between the two opposed, though not antagonistic, poles of his particular poetic preciousness — namely an almost fleshy expansion of the form and refined modelling — and comes to rest on ever different points of balance. Later he reached a more detached vision, and turned from mythical atmosphere to fable. Amongst the works reproduced here, two, belonging to one of the most successful years of his activity, 1956, represent the extremities of the curve of his art. The *Crouching*

Pl. XXXVI *Figure* has soft plastic fullness of form, and translates his sense of warm and expansive carnality into figurative terms (not merely flatly imitative ones). Such fullness would be almost excessive, had not the artist made a kind of parallelogram of the chaste pose of the figure, thus keeping it within a strict, though not cramping, spatial design; it is in an area

Pl. XXXV of dreaming meditation all of its own. In the *Large Bather,* on the other hand, it is immediately clear that, as Carli says, " the rounded firmness of the volumes... is the extreme limit of a dynamic impulse seeking to free itself from the interior of the figure, but which has been forced into an impenetrable case by the artist ". But then we discover, especially looking at the figure from behind, how this closed volumetric continuity is subtly altered, for refined, linear cadences show through, like delicate arabesques. Greco here is a mannerist, and suggestions of sixteenth-century Mannerism have been found in certain of his ways of solving problems of form. For Mascherini this served both as a kind of semantic limit and a syntax for his language of pastoral lyricism, but for Greco it represents the most pleasant way of going from nature to fable. Therefore it is not surprising that one of his

Pl. XXXVII best works — with a more difficult theme — is the *Monument to Pinocchio*. Carli rightly points out that the figures come into being at the end of a development of spiral planes, and the volume opens up to receive space (in an original, not a servile version of wide-

24

spread themes of modern sculpture), and that there is "an imaginative airiness, not of lines, but of robust and strongly defined volumes of carefully calculated thicknesses, which free themselves in a bold and inexhaustible drive towards open space, in victory over the light which envelopes them, gets in amongst them, almost becomes entangled with them, but is unable to penetrate or cleave them ". These volumes include, surround, and absorb, but do not abolish those tender and delicate falling lines to which the projection of the images into the world of a smiling or melancholy fairy tale is chiefly confided. It is precisely here, where the " manneristic " refinements are expressed in the most modern structural language, that the sensual warmth is all poured away and dissolves into a sweet and modulated elegy in which once more — in spite of the very different spirit of the human but easy Tuscan tale — a faint and subtle nostalgia for a subdued Hellenic beauty seems to come to flower.

There are other sculptors of the middle generation, with a more traditional attitude, in the sense that with them the virtue of noble fidelity to their art is stronger than the fervour of formal imagination. They are at work today on a cultural plane which, because of its archaic or classical reminiscences, can in some way be set on the same level as that of the masters we are discussing. One of these is Adriano Alloati the younger, who must be given credit for having come through unharmed from the vanity of the triumphal rhetoric of the last, outworn period of the *Novecento*, even though he received a typically academic education. With great tenacity and fidelity to himself he went on to develop from the professional realism of his origins towards a bucolic naturalism, and his postwar works give clear evidence of this. The female nude, as exemplified in the *Naiads*, is his recurrent Pl. XXXIX, XL subject, and the one that best throws light upon the processes of his art. The natural material is gradually overcome by form, but the form still retains the vital breath of nature, and itself reshapes the other forms according to the dictates of the artist's imagination, which is turned towards the evocative and the fabulous.

Dante Zamboni was also trained and developed during those same difficult times in honest fidelity to himself and to tradition, the sources of which he seeks especially in the Renaissance — but (it must be observed) more in the irregular rather than the classical aspects of that golden period. There is no secret about his admiration for the mythological devilries of Riccio of Padua, and proof is in the *Rape of the Nymph*. It corresponds Pl. XLI moreover to his taste for springing, muscular and sinewy forms, which are defined by a line that it is not too much to call functional, as in the *Dancer*. In brief, there is Pl. XLII continual striving towards greater and greater vibrant vitality.

All these sculptors seek inspiration in an archaic or classical past. But other artists could be termed Realists, provided the term is used with the necessary caution.

Fig. 9 - *Lorenzo Pepe* (1912): Donkey, bronze, 1956.

I do not intend to limit myself to the type of realism seeking its justification in a well defined ideological system, but I include those artists who look directly at reality and set themselves in front of it in a more or less openly moderate state of mind. In this group the first rank goes to Pericle Fazzini. As a very young man, about 1930, he began to frequent the circle of " Young Turks " — Scipione, Mafai, Mazzacurati, Antonietta Raphaël — which, with the so called " Roman " school, represented a valid antithesis to the *Novecento* and an open door, or a least a half-open door, for the artistic currents of Europe to enter. It was a complex movement, in which neo-romantic, expressionist and realist trends existed side by side, or merged. The carnal and pathetic realism seeking expression in the anguished painting and sculpture of the Lithuanian Antonietta Raphaël

Pl. XLIII   certainly contributed towards orientating Fazzini towards an attitude of outright sincerity and immediate contact with reality: a reality sensed above all in its heaviness and massive power, like a squared block (even in a material as difficult to mould as wood). He brings out the importance and urgency of the energy that is pressing heavily from inside. His *Dance* reliefs (wood) and the *Storm* (stone) of 1934 are now famous. The physical movement in them is baulked by the opposition of immobile masses; it is

26

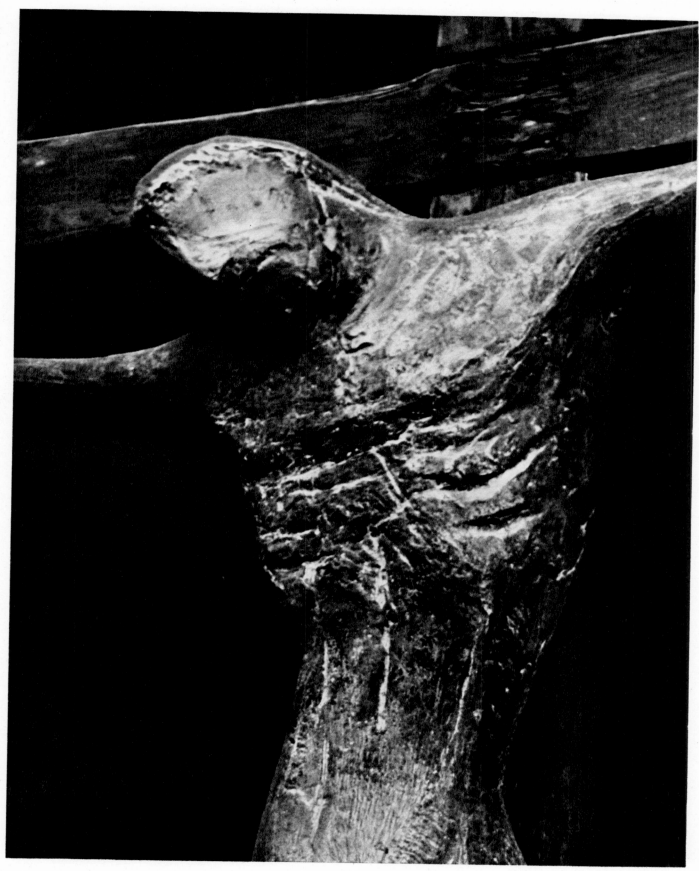

Fig. 10 - Alfio Castelli (1917): *Crucifixion* (detail), marble, 1956.

an enclosed but explosive power. In the *Portrait of Ungaretti* (1936) " the carved wood has been scratched and cut, there are wedges in it, plugs, splits, breaks, crevices, knots come to flower, and all keep the sense of creation alive: and the subject... is caught with incisive realism, with no uncertainties or formal sophistries " (De Micheli). That is to say that the spiritual force that the artist intuitively perceives in his model is translated into the invincible power of the material, which is still crude and roughly carved, but is absorbing and transforming the eruptive forces of the spirit into its own formal language. It is not surprising that Fazzini should have rediscovered the nude as his essential theme — after the first experiments of the already mentioned *Dance* and similar works, and the rather episodic deviation of his *Anita* of 1939. His nudes, full of a solid sense of the flesh, are without sensual incitement. In them the flesh is expressed in rounded and very close volumes, gathered into richly contrasted compositions. Their sane and intense vitality ab-

Pl. XLVI   sorbs and raises up the spiritual substance of man. Thus in the *Acrobats* of 1948 (plaster), it is not so much the bold invention that matters, as the discipline existing in the play of the rounded volumes, which swell with fleshly vigour, and the closed construction, which is solid and has perfect equilibrium. Unbridled vitality is transformed into controlled

Pl. XLIV   energy. In the *Sibyl* of 1947 (bronze) a plastic nude form, rounded and firmly fleshed, is disciplined by extremely sharp contour outlines, and this discipline culminates in the very restrained form of the head, which is cut in triangular shape, and to which the triangle of the supporting arm corresponds; the head itself is wedged into the larger triangle of the cap. Thus these rounded, almost bloated forms do not expand, but enclose and lock themselves in a compact and impenetrable block.

His figures give the feeling of indomitable force, which will not break out, but remain shut in the finely moulded forms as the perennial principle of life. This explains their almost ritual solemnity, and why the *Acrobats* in the closed continuity of their rhythm seem to be carrying out the ritual of some nature religion, and the *Sibyl*, as Ungaretti has written, becomes " an idol beyond all time and space, enclosing within itself, in its tremendous impenetrability, all time and all space, in firm, ever youthful flesh ". A symbolic expression of this mysteriously perennial life-force is perhaps to be found in his figures of cats. They are motionless and as mysterious as sphinxes, and whether up on their paws to watch the movements of the prey or scratching their ears with almost acrobatic gestures, they are always very far from yielding to the vanity of episodic naturalism. No concession of any kind is made to *genre* in the recent figures of the *Boy in the Sun* and the *Squatting Boy*. These figures give form to a sun myth of mysterious and everlasting Life, because the plasticity of their volume is absolutely compact and their otherwise complex composition is completely unified.

Fig. 11 - Bruno Calvani (1904): *Pulcinella*, bronze, 1955.

Marino Mazzacurati is considered today as the standard-bearer of Neo-realism, by which is meant ideologically and polemically engaged Realism.

The coherence of his efforts cannot be denied — from the time when, already mature, he first became a sculptor (he was formerly engaged in drawing and painting), up to his more recent works. This coherence applies more to the intentions than to the achievements or artistic substance of his work. He showed admirable constancy in setting himself to overcome his obvious academic beginnings (in the sense of the polish and finesse of his craft and his artistic concepts). From time to time, expressionist or cubist shoots have been grafted on, and from Arturo Martini he derived his lack of prejudice in regard to varying his subject matter and form, thus fairly soon reaching an outright anti-academic attitude. But this attitude has not taken the shape of definite artistic tenets, but expresses itself in ironic criticism of society and manners. From time to time, he has vented this expressionistically, *Portrait of the Count* (1936), or has used Cubism, *Figure of a Man* (1944-7), or the most uninhibited Verismo, in *The Emperors*, or *The Massacre of the Innocents* (1942), where he attains a grotesque effect in the manner of Grosz, in which it is easy to read a protest against Fascism and its war. The protest does not turn into poetry, however, but into lucid satire in cubist-like language, as if Picasso's *Guernica* were translated " into plastic terms deduced from an inverted classicism, in which the ' heroic ' nudes become deformed, gross bodies, and the fury of the massacre becomes obscene

Pl. XLVII, XLVIII revelry" (Maltese). More recently, in the *Monument to the Resistance*, the sculptor has been able to get away from satire and call on other feelings, creating a work of lyrical and pathetic realism, which almost attains the full liberty of the lyrical image because of the grandeur of the effort of composition and the unity obtained by means of a parabolic trajectory on the horizontal; but it is hindered by episodic description which too seldom rises above the requirements of photographic realism.

Oscar Gallo's training was in the traditional Verismo of Evaristo Boncinelli, but he moved away from it by taking part in the activity of the *frondisti* (frondeurs) with Maccari, and joining in the artistic atmosphere about Rosai at Florence. His is a simple naturalism without theoretical basis. It is spontaneous and seems to rise from a natural agreement in his imagination between exact perception of reality and the exigencies of severe formal

Pl. XLIX, L discipline. Thus, in the heads reproduced here, the firm construction is immediately evident but does not affect the robust pulsation of the soft, breathing forms apparently able to transfer their vital inner warmth to the clay. In other words, the material seems to be slowly leavened, until by its own power it is adequate to meet the demands of great formal clarity. From this subdued struggle he derives that meditative and recollected tone in which the tranquil figures exist. Between 1930 and 1940 Realism of the Left — in oppo-

Fig. 12 - Carlo Conte (1898): *Woman Twisting Her Hair*, bronze, 1941.

sition to the classicizing realism of the regime — Expressionism and Post-Impressionism were the systems entwining and merging in the circles of the more gifted young artists, and they all contributed to the crisis of the *Novecento*.

The anti-*Novecento fronde* assumed a particulary neo-romantic colour in the Milanese movement of *Corrente* (from 1938 to 1943 : their review of the same name was suppressed by the political police in 1940). Proof is to be found in the works of Luigi Broggini, one of the few sculptors amongst them, who had sought inspiration at Paris from the

Pl. LI, LII Impressionism of Degas and Renoir, also from the ideas of Grandi, Rosso and Aligi Sassu. But Broggini could infuse subtler and more sinewy vibration into his work, and this has

Fig. 15 led him to the frontiers of Expressionism, especially in his most recent productions. Sassu, however, went back more directly — since he is above all a painter — to Delacroix and Géricault. His cyclists, harlequins and horses are intensely pictorial, tonal sculptures, and are alive with intense, fantastic dynamism. At Rome, too, some artists took this road, as in the case of Leoncillo, whose temperament has greater and more exceptional gifts and poetic capacities than many others, and who has found the suitable language for them in sculptural and polychrome ceramics. In his youthful works, from 1935 on, he renders the whirling and dramatic expressionism of Scipione with a simplifying, almost rococo lightness of touch, and in deformed figures of ancient mythology (Harpies, Sirens, Hermaphrodites) he gives expression to his feeling for a bizarre (and somewhat sinister) mystery of life. The romantic and dramatic spirit of his vision is more evident in the works which in 1943 and 1944 were inspired by the Resistance, and reaches its culmination in the *Monument to the Women Partisans of the Veneto* (1955-6) in a language that has been enriched by his knowledge of Picassan Neo-Cubism. In his latest works the human figure is abandoned, for, absorbed in his feeling of uneasy astonishment at bizarre and incomprehensible reality, Leoncillo has arrived at forms which bring him closer to the practitioners of abstract art and of the "informal" observance.

This was not a premeditated, but an instinctive conclusion, enabling him to benefit

Pl. LIII, LIV from all the advantages of spontaneous expression. His recent *Tagli* (free pieces) join luminous and explosive colour effects obtained with enamel and other highly developed technical procedures to the fragmentary and splintered character of forms that seem unwilling to accept a clear-cut situation in space. In the end these works express the obscure vitality of the material and also the unquiet, dramatic wonder of the artist, who feels nature as a depository of magical powers. In the singular personality of Leoncillo expressionistic, informal and surrealistic tendencies meet as at a crossroad.

Minguzzi is another who is now definitely moving towards the abstract, guided by expressionistic impulses which from the beginning of his artistic life infused a restless and

32

Fig. 13 - Quinto Martini (1908): *The Cook*, bronze, 1960.

almost rebellious spirit into his sculptures, originally inspired by the tender forms of Manzù. After the war the artist came into close contact with the most modern aspects of European sculpture, from the latest Martini to Picasso, and in the liberty of invention suggested by these experiences he found a more suitable language for his fiery and vital temperament. His true maturity begins about 1950 with that series of animals, " the terrible, sheer physical force and vital tension of which are exalted and made giant-like in the closed architectural structure of the forms " (Gnudi). His Expressionism, however, is free of the pessimistic vision and tragic sense of slavery and abjection characteristic of the German school of that name, and is turned rather towards catching life in its moments of most intense and even pointless energy, including even grotesque features. Thus, in the *Dog Among Reeds* of 1951 the cage imprisoning the animal does not give the idea of tragic oppression, but makes a contrast to the leaping energy of the vigorous plasticity of the figure. *The Contortionist*, 1952, is deformed, but the shapes are full and solid, and perhaps owe something to Fazzini. They are not there to introduce features of dramatic conflict, but to emphasize the heaviness—which for Minguzzi signifies liberty — of the tensed, vital

Pl. LVIII energy. Also, in the later *Prisoner of War*, the precisely modelled forms and the harshly intersecting wire serve as an abstraction of the vital energy of the imprisoned figure which has been stretched to the utmost. Little by little Minguzzi was thus able to give more subtlety to the subject content of his figures until he reached a kind of evocative abstraction,

Pl. LVII as in the *Shadows In the Wood* (1956), where a wire arrangement suggesting the tangled boughs of the trees rises up over a system of forms, human only by association, not merely in order to agree with the title, but also so as to give the luminous, nervous linear restlessness of the "figures" a subtler vibrancy, and restless, intangible mobility. He moved from the still allusive abstract art of the human figures, the two light and dancing *Shadows*

Pl. LV (1957), on to completely abstract works (which nevertheless retain expressionistic tenden-
Pl. LVI cies): *Two Forms* and the series of *Kites*.

Mirko's expressionism has not hidden his tendency to surrealism. A pupil of Arturo Martini, he inherited his taste for myth and the primordial spirit, but the anti-classical element in his work is a taste for the form, not for the ideological content of Expressionism, and it acts by deforming the subject. His youthful figures of minotaurs, cyclops and chimeras are given shape in a language of intense and highly mobile pictorial qualities and sinewy linear vibration which all strive to recover a primordial and prehistoric sense of life. But this primordial spirit was not understood in an historical or prehistoric sense, but as a symbol of the obscure origins of life. A complete example is to be found in the *Chimera* (1954), where the obsessive prominence of the monstrous shape and the orientalizing forms stamped upon it correspond to that sense of the formlessness of matter

34

Fig. 14 - Giuseppe Scalvini (1908): *Offering*, bronze, 1957.

Fig. 15 - Aligi Sassu (1912): *Rearing Horse*, bronze, 1958.

Fig. 16 - Vittorio Tavernari (1919): *Three Figures*, concrete, 1958.

which the bronze retains. The conglomeration of these forms in a compact mass roughen-ed by the imprint of a mysterious alphabet, crystallizes the idea of life arising from shapeless matter, which in its turn is identified with the mysterious depths of the un-conscious. Mirko had already given expression to surrealistic tendencies, in a quite un-usual way, in the three gates of the *Mausoleum of the Fosse Ardeatine* at Rome. " They were imagined and composed first of all as figured bas-reliefs with crowded groups of figures in low relief (armed partisans, people, angels and palms as symbols of glory)... but in later stages of the project they were more and more deprived of all historical charac-teristics and stripped of naturalistic elements, which in the end were entirely translated (though not suppressed) into absolutely abstract language " (Martinelli).

Pl. LX

This is evidently not a case of doctrinaire abstraction purporting to express the artist's feeling in forms stripped of all representative value — as if it were possible to write poetry with meaningless words — but is a descent from the realm of the image born in light down to the dark and hidden places of the unconscious, where violence and revolt, oppression and redemption are all perceived in a twilight region at the roots of the deepest and most obscure movements of the human soul. The powerful dramatic entanglement of these forms seems to express a tragedy that has its source in the obscure origins of life. From an awareness of man's subjection to obscure ancestral forces is born that sense of anguish dominating his magical figure creations of *Warriors* or the *Warrior Dances*, mysterious and terrible totems where movements of the soul stemming from a vision of life that may be associated with modern existentialist thought are clothed in images of primordial mythology.

Pl. LXI, LIX

Of all our sculptors Mirko is the one that has gone most fully into the possibilities of a surrealist artistic theory, and has most deepened our understanding of it, for he em-braced it not merely out of intellectual conviction, but because he discovered it at the end of a long road travelled because of a spontaneous need for expression.

Other sculptors have also called at the island of Surrealism: Agenore Fabbri, for instance, with his howling dogs, great birds, fighting animals, and men struggling with beasts. His lean expressionistic language delves deep into instinctive life, felt as elementary, sinister violence; and in works like the *Big Bird* (1956), *The Man of Tomorrow* (1958) and *The Bird* (1960), he attains an even more basic expressive language by means of strident forms and a spirit of ferocity that seem to spring from the darkest depths of the unconscious as a monstrous dream symbol.

Pl. LXIII, LXIV

Raffaello Salimbeni succeeds in expressing his surrealistic tendencies through the dominant note of his work, which is an almost Kafkan bitterness at the spectacle of the alienation of man. In the sketch for the *Monument to the Political Prisoner* (1952) the

38

Fig. 17 - Carlo Russo: *Dancing Figure*, terracotta, 1960.

human figures are flattened, smoothed out, and stretched forward, their insect-like bodies measuring out in all directions a spatial network of circles and barbed hooks, that absorb the whole space instead of breaking off a section of it. It is as if through the rotation of these circles he sought to express the absurd vision of a universe become an immense iron prison. His art expresses the bitterness of a humanity that has become alienated because it is constrained by mysterious and therefore uncontrollable forces. The series

Pl. LXVI of *Woman with a Fan*, which seems to derive from his amused observation of an innocent custom, culminates, in the example reproduced here, in a vision of bitter humour, clothed in the Kafka fancy of a human being metamorphosed into an insect. Here, too, the surrealistic accent is already present, and it deepens in his most recent works. No one will

Pl. LXV deny the surrealism in the firmly designed but wholly vibrant form of the *Space Man* (1960), where the images of modern science fiction merge with atavistic memories of the ancient figure of the angel. The result is sorrowing astonishment at the mysterious magic that transforms man into a powerful but inhuman machine. In the sad vibrancy of the lines and the excitedly clashing planes woven together into a solid organism, he expresses once more, but this time with a streak of humour, his state of profoundly sensitive bitterness at the contrast between his nostalgic aspiration towards classical and human beauty of form and the obscure and irresistible feeling of the inevitable corruption of all things and the disturbing alienation of man.

The still recent sculptural activity of Chió deserves special mention because of the unusual route by which he came to sculpture after decades of painting and drawing, and because he is self-taught and an improviser. Anyone looking through the albums of his drawings of the Maremma heathlands will see that his artistic activity arose from the ned to clothe his love for his adopted home in acute, witty and astonished images.

He feels the presence of mythical antiquity in the Maremma, as also in his native

Pl. LXVII, LXVIII Tuscan Valdarno (where admirable fossils are preserved). The fish and birds, with which he is chiefly concerned, have something about them of the millenary antiquity of fossils and the instinctive vitality of nature, exactly like the Maremma, which he feels as a land of vast antiquity and unspoiled nature.

We must now turn our attention to those artistic currents that more or less closely derive from the theory — or theories — of abstract art, and which occupy so much space in the panorama of contemporary sculpture no less than in contemporary painting. Pride of place is undoubtedly due to Lucio Fontana, because of his seniority, the fervour of his work, and his inspired invention. Towards 1930, aged thirty, he was drawing human and animal figures on boards, taking his inspiration from the mural paintings in prehistoric caves. Some of these panels already bear abstract designs, and lively and variously shaped

40

forms were cut, coloured on the flat, and then raised on a pedestal to be presented already at this date as the artist's earliest abstract sculptures. This abstract art is not derived from Cubism, even though the artist is *au courant* with that movement. His forms dart up like tongues of flame and seek to penetrate space, in spite of their almost completely two dimensional limits, and unceasingly strive to conquer light. Delicate pennons are grafted on to even more delicate laths of plaster or even coloured cement — and the general effect is to stress the empty spaces, as if to indicate that form and space interpenetrate. There have been times when he has worked primarily at figurative art, in polychrome ceramics — like the *Portrait of Paulette* (1936), in which the artist takes the graceful lightness of Rococo as his starting point, abstracts it from its own involved lines, and makes the in- Fig. 18 tensely coloured, corroded and seething forms vibrate in a space that is also light. In all these sculptures there is an impulse to dissolve the limits of form and the earthly bounds of things into the immense liberty of space. The impulse is potentially a lyric one, but it remains generalized, and does not succeed in expressing a definite sentiment or producing a concrete image. The same enormous thematic dispersion is evident once again in the artist's anguished, certainly sincere, but vain attempt to define an image, or a series of images capable of incorporating his artistic inspirations. His various productions are united by a thread of easy ornamental grace, which associates them all on the decorative plane. After the war, in the *Manifestos of Spatial Art*, Fontana developed a theory for the concepts already implicit throughout his preceding work, starting from the principle of a necessary parallel between the development of science and the development of art. Baroque art was born when, in the seventeenth and eighteenth centuries, physics for the first time reveal-ed the nature of dynamics, and found that motion "is a condition immanent in matter as a principle of the comprehension of the universe". The notion of time was united to sculp-tural art, for the figures seem to abandon their planes and the depicted movements are continued into space. Today, since with the discovery of new physical forces the mastery of matter and of space is gradually imposing conditions upon man that never existed be-fore in his history, " it is necessary to tread the open road of Futurism and to undertake the development of an art based on the unity of time and space ", one made up of " a sum of the physical elements: colour, sound, motion, space, all integrated in ideal and material unity ". Colour, the element of space, sound, the element of time, and motion, which de-velops in both time and space, are the fundamentals of the new art, which thus contains the four dimensions of existence. The application of this programme, as far as pos-sible, was attempted by Fontana in 1949 in the *Spatial Environment* in the *Galleria del Naviglio*, and resulted in an interesting scenographic production. But the application to sculpture was even more difficult, and the artist had to content himself with creating a

41

series symbolizing his thirst for space. From 1949 onwards we get the "spatial concepts", which consist of great white canvases with rhythmical series of craterform openings arranged upon them in circles and ellipses. According to one of the artist's many apologists these are meant to represent "the magic rhythm of astral spaces, the mystery of the vacuum that is the mystery of the universe". But really we discern only a certain feeling for the most elementary of rhythms, and at most a pale representation of the starry sky (farewell, abstract art!). These works may be appreciated as studies in decorative ideas, and indeed the most valid results are to be found in certain very beautiful plates marked with ink spots and deformed concentric circles. More recent "spatial concepts" bear the title of

Pl. LXX *Expectation* (*Attesa*) and consist of areas of coloured and extended canvas, which occasionally assume, as in the example reproduced here, the form of rather regular pentagons, and on this immaculate surface a clear, clean, bright fissure is opened (sometimes more than one). These are luminous fields upon which the eye willingly rests, and we can also notice, quoting another, often very acute interpreter of the artist, that "the fissure always falls on the right point, obeying the necessity of breaking the perfect plane, as if the material had been brought to the extreme limit of rarefaction, and now wished to recover the sense of the reality of its own existence in this detail" (Argan). But when Argan goes on to say that this piece is "a furrow, in the earth or in a woman, and puts the earthly or human surface in communication with the profound inscrutable spatiality of the creativity of the cosmos", we can only agree if this is understood as allegorically, even analogically, superimposed, and not necessarily contained in the literal significance of the form. Here we have neither image nor poetry, but an ornamented cryptograph of extreme simplicity or, to avoid a single term, decoration and symbol. But the result is not yet art. The latest discovery of this untiring inventor is another series of

Pl. LXIX "spatial concepts" called *Natures*: great wrinkled balls in ceramic or sandstones, like pomegranates opening at the top in a kind of crater. And these objects are also meant to be symbols of sex and fecundity, as the name given them by their creator indicates, and as authoritative interpreters confirm. They appear in isolation sometimes, and at other times are disseminated in circular fashion on the flat or plane of a pavement or sort of bowl. Proper admiration for their author's inventive fertility and valuable and refined craftsmanship is one thing, but to describe these productions as works of art is quite another, just as invention and ornamentation are one thing and imagination another. To try to justify them with a definition of art as the production of "things that are also signs" is a matter of speculative subtlety, falling into paradox. It would mean transferring the alphabet to the region of art, and road sign too, because in the case we are considering the transmission "of the rhythm of space into the smallest forms of existence" (this is claimed

42

Fig. 18 - Lucio Fontana (1899): *Crucifixion*, ceramic, 1948.

to be the conceptual content of these works) is not really verifiable in the object itself, that is, is not expressed by it, but is simply deduced from the artist's theoretical statements and from the arguments of his interpreters and apologists.

Fontana's " spatial " abstracts are thus mainly interesting for historical reasons as evidence of a widespread desire to keep art apace with science, in accordance with the problem posed by Futurism; and his work shares this characteristic with several other sculptors. One of these is Mino Rosso, a tenacious elaborator of futuristic forms. He sometimes openly attaches himself to Boccioni — as in *Elements in Flight* (1927) — or seeks to render the heavy rhythms of the populist expressionism of Sironi and Permeke in almost abstract volumes; finally, in his most recent attempts — as in the *Portrait of*

Fig. 20 *Arpino* (1960) — he seems to have returned to the origins of the avant-garde, combining subtleties in the Art Nouveau manner with moderate cubistic dismemberment. Umberto Mastroianni is a true Neo-futurist, and it is characteristic of him that he followed the same road as Boccioni to some degree, after an academic education received from Guerrisi, and found his own language rather late, at the end of the war. Like Boccioni he feels life as dynamism, but for him dynamism is inherent in matter. So his problem is to charge matter with force without rarefying it, but even enhancing its closed compactness, and to make use of it as a hammer or wedge to repel space. For him space is absolutely negative, life is all a matter of volume, and volume is just the form of dynamic matter. His

Pl. LXXI figures appear to have crystallized from an explosion brought about by the force of an indomitable cohesive power in the material. They still preserve some vague reminiscent connec-

Pl. LXXII tion with reality, but sometimes depart from it entirely. Nevertheless, it has been observed that "his form, although essentially abstract, has so great a human element in it that it frequently seems to be representational. His men and women are different from those we know in reality, but they are under the influence of such a differentiated breath of passion, such an individual one, that it is easy to identify the human image behind the artistic screen " (Venturi). Otherwise, as Masciotta's clear and sensible exposition of the sculptor's imaginative and work processes shows, Mastroianni proceeds by a series of figures, one deriving from the other through analysis and recomposition of the preceding figures. That is to say, he starts by setting up a determined subject, which he then forms and reforms into figures, taking the preceding figure as the material for the next. The subject once having been found, he has to unwind its dynamic components and strip them more and more, so as to arrive finally at the most coherent possible glorification of the at once explosive and cohesive life-force of matter. It is beyond doubt that these productions

44

attain the status of artistic images, because their language expresses the dramatic pathos informing the artist's vision without any need for superimposed symbols.

The abstract art of Somaini is also of Cubist origin, but includes Expressionist tendencies. He was able originally to benefit from a study of Arp and Moore, but his geometric formalism proper to the concepts of Cubism dissolves under the influence of authentic inspiration. Indeed, "Somaini's problem is not to produce sculpture wich closed, contemplated and volumetric forms, but to create variously shaped planes from which space rebounds like a voice striking a wall and reverberating in the echo" (Apollonio). This means that the sculpture exists in a dialectic of form and space. But the forms take concrete shape in iron — even when the artist uses bronze it looks like iron — which is rough and torn and assumes the appearance of fossils. (We are reminded that Somaini's modern development began in 1945 with a series of studies of animal skulls.) The fact is that the powerful development of his helicoid forms expresses the artist's struggle for the conquest of space and a sense of primordial, vital power, but at the same time he seeks the origins of this obscure power of expansion in the bowels of the earth, mythologically understood as the repository and conserver in its age-old womb of every principle and every vital form. It is exactly the series of helicoidal forms of about 1955 that seems to me to represent the highest point of this sculptor's production, for it immediately transmits his sense of the expansion in light of a life that has been excavated from the darkest recesses of the earth. In his work during more recent years, following a series of exercises on spirals and helicoids in the vertical, the figures evoke human shapes in tones varying from the fiery vehemence of *Absalom* to the suffering maceration of *Martyrdom*. Perhaps the balance between the human feelings evoked and the fossil-like material in which they are embodied still awaits ultimate clarification. But quite clearly Somaini is guided by the force of a passionate search to disinter life from deep layers and to bring human emotions of deep antiquity into our present, almost as if to bear witness to the eternity of the human situation.

Pl. LXXIV

Pl. LXXIII

Pietro Consagra was among the promoters of the "Form" group at Rome soon after its liberation in 1944. This movement desired to concretize Marxism's strivings towards social renewal and undertook bold formalistic researches, starting substantially from that equation of revolution = avant-garde that had a brief career in Russia after the October Revolution. Hence a certain orientation towards Russian Constructivism and, through affinity with this, towards Futurism. The resulting abstract art corresponds to the artist's declared intention of expressing "the dramatic rhythm of life today in sculptural elements that will be the formal synthesis of man's actions in his relation to the workings of our society, where will, strength, optimism, simplicity and clarity are necessities ". His abstract art will therefore be " engaged ", and indeed the most frequent title that he

45

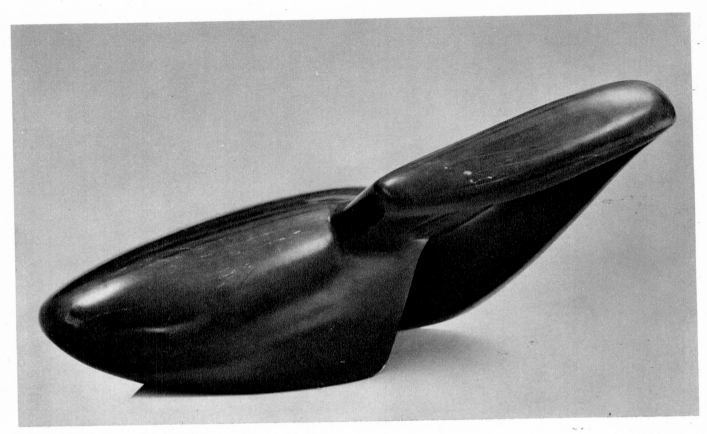

Fig. 19 - Carlo Sergio Signori (1906): *Reclining Venus*, marble, 1959.

Pl. LXXV, LXXVI gives to his sculptures is *Dialogue* (*Colloquio*). It is not difficult to see that by means of the lacerated and pitted surfaces of these great strips of bronze, with their torn outlines, or the axes of splintered, incised and pyrographed wood, the sculptor wishes to project the outline of an excited discourse of dialectical clash onto the plane, as if onto a screen.

Thus, his formless sheets sometimes seem to take on human vitality. Nevertheless, as De Micheli has pointed out, the necessity of very exact sculptural definition is met, not by indications from the figure itself, but by too vague an aesthetic emotion.

But this conclusion may be applied to many other artists with abstractionist tendencies, and undoubtedly derives from the difficulty (or absurdity) of coining a language which shall be purely expressive and without semantic content — like a soul without a body. This can be said, too, of Berto Ladera, who also starts out from a constructivist conception and, through a series of compositions of crescent-shaped sheets intersecting on the plane or in Pl. LXXVII, LXXVIII right-angled encounters in space, seeks to express a sense of harshly clashing forces, with effects not dissimilar from those obtained in painting by Magnelli, whose dominant influence he may have felt during a long stay in Paris. The sculpture of Umberto Milani, on the other hand, is characterized by highly refined symbolism. He has abandoned cubist Pl. LXXIX, LXXX problems, which he explored until 1952. On sheets of plaster, cement, or bronze, sometimes recalling fragments from an excavation and at other times forms of musical instru-

46

Fig. 20 - Mino Rosso (1904): *Portrait of Giovanni Arpino,* bronze, 1960.

Pl. LXXXI,
LXXXII

Pl. LXXXIII,
LXXXIV

Fig. 21

Pl. LXXXV,
LXXXVI

Fig. 23

ments, he stamps the signs of a secret alphabet, whose power of suggestion derives sometimes from the evocation of ancient Celtic coins and sometimes from the reminiscence of the sliding of a bow over the strings of a 'cello. In the recent work of Carmelo Capello, there is something of hermetic symbolism, characterized by bronze arabesques, which free themselves lightly into the air, drawing tender and capricious fantastic shapes, while the productions of Nino Franchina are not without deeper surrealistic significance, as also is the work of Aldo Calò who, after having attempted to infuse the pure sensualism of marine forms with mysterious meaning, is now engaged in working out Moore's geological primitivism in a surrealistic way. Carlo Ramous looks back to Moore as to Marini, and a successive examination of three of his works, *Two Figures* (1957), the *Dialogue* (1958) and the *Dance under the Full Moon* (1960) show well enough the direction he is taking. He began by assimilating the human figure to rock, and has ended by merging man, animal and nature in a single form, characterized by heavy immobility and mute and weighty monumentality. Perhaps there is also a tendency towards a poetical feeling of wonder at the material having remained inert from millenary antiquity.

Only some aspects of the thin succession of sculptures deriving from the work of Arturo Martini touch on abstract art. Thus Bertagnin passes from the archaizing *Shipwreck* (1950) in Martini's manner, to the grandiose form of the *Cow Licking Itself* (1957), in which Martini's impetuous naturalism yields to a kind of silent monumentality; in the *Cloaked Woman* (1959) he seeks to draw deeper meanings from the impressionistic vision of a great cloak blown about by the wind.

Fig. 24

In his field, which has been called " abstract-concrete ", we also find the art of one of the more important of today's sculptors, Alberto Viani. He was a pupil of Arturo Martini, and was open to the Cubist experiences of Brancusi and Arp, and was also an admirer of late archaic Greek sculpture. But he has created his own unmistakable language. His story begins in 1945 with the *Female Torso* in the Museum of Modern Art, New York. It lacks head, arms and legs, but we do not have the impression that it is only a fragment, because a plastic roundness closes the forms in unitary and self-sufficient rhythm. Using the free invention learnt from Martini and with the help of Brancusi's and Arp's geometrics, Viani takes the scale of proportions of an ancient torso and renders them in forms which expand in space and present themselves to us with authority as the units of the measure of human beauty. Though tending to be abstract, they are still representative, because they preserve the pulsation, the warmth and sensuous softness of the female body, felicitously reduced to their essentials. Later his forms are shaped in plaster or sculptured in a highly polished marble — it might have been smoothed by the action of some fresh

Pl. XC

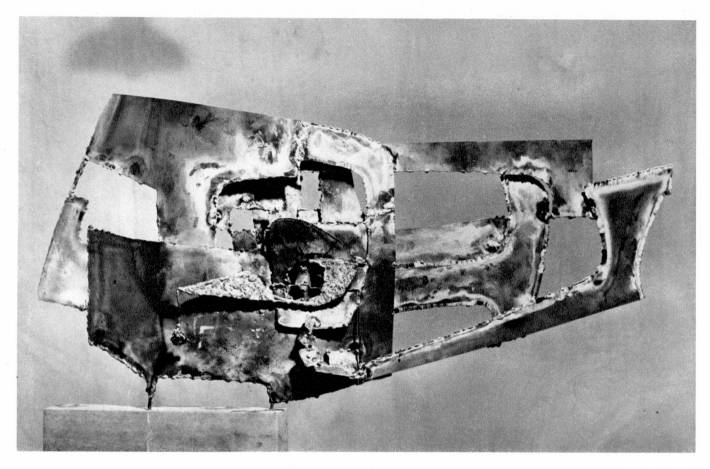

Fig. 21 - Edgardo Mannucci (1904): *Idea No. 12*, bronze, 1960.

mountain stream — and they take on a lustre which puts us in mind of the neo-classical Pl. LXXXIX refinement of Canova (Viani comes from the same region). But there is no neo-classical frigidity in Viani's art. On the contrary, we do not get an impression of gradual transition from natural forms to geometric ones by a process of abstraction, but the opposite, almost as if an elemental vital urge were taking concrete shape through its tendency to become a natural object. His sense of the warm and luminous vitality of the human body remains alive as his lines and planes develop and form the outline of a "circular" melody. The sinuous and agile course of the line cannot really be distinguished from the equally delicate and swift variations of the sculptural planes. The universal validity of this concept is confirmed by the fact that the third dimension is not present in these works as a premise or category of space, but is inseparable from the trajectory described by the lines and planes. Thus, highly felicitous and absolutely coherent figures express his candid emotion at the spectacle of a world where the sensuous movement of physical life is celebrated in pure forms and is identified with the ideal of the most abstract and pure beauty. The plaster of 1958 represents perhaps the highest point the artist has reached in this direction. Pl. LXXXVII We can enjoy the helicoid development of those very pure planes in the light as decoration because of their formal beauty, but we understand their deepest significance when

Fig. 22 - Franco Garelli (1909): *The Host*, bronze, 1960.

Fig. 23 - Carlo Ramous (1926): *Dance in the Full Moon*, bronze, 1960.

Fig. 24 - Roberto Bertagnin (1914): *Cloaked Woman*, bronze, 1959.

we catch their still vivid resemblance to a nude dancing woman. It is exactly this underlying dialectic between fresh, natural and joyous vitality and the stainless purity of the forms that gives birth to the poetical image: a wonderful equation between the movement of life and the brightness of light.

Many promising sculptors from the younger generation — born about 1930 — could be mentioned, but there would be little new to say with regard to future developments and new directions in the artistic search. Most of them, though not lacking in talent, still seem to be bound up with academic abstractionism. Thus Gio Pomodoro oscillates between the vaguely abstract Expressionism of the splintered forms of this school in his *Crowd* and an effort to express the wondering luminosity of the highly smoothed and polished,

Pl. XCI

52

Fig. 25 - Mario Negri (1916): *Large Multiple Figure*, bronze, 1957.

PI. XCII scarcely modulated planes of *Co-existence*. Perhaps some sculptors in the figurative tradition show more promise, and among these I should like to mention Augusto Perez, who modelled himself on Greco, but tends to render the master's evocative Hellenism in a PI. XCIII, XCIV lower and more populist tone. Instead of Greco's secure sense of plastic arrangement we find in this sculptor a certain tendency towards soft pictoriality, by means of which he succeeds not only in cancelling the sheen of the planes and forms, but also almost in breaking them up, and thus penetrating into the form itself. His projection of the world of dreams and fables into his figures is facilitated by this means.

We do not wish to draw particular conclusions from this brief review. It is still too early to find a logical thread of development running through the multiple and contradictory aspects of the sculpture of this century. We can only declare that Italian sculpture has offered, and still has to offer, a number of authentic artistic values, and also has shared, and continues in often original ways to share, in the problems of European art of our time. And so in the field of sculpture, also, Italy's provincial isolation has become but a distant memory.

ROBERTO SALVINI

PLATES

Pl. I - Umberto Boccioni (1882-1916): *Muscles in Rapid Action*, bronze, 1913.

Pl. II - Umberto Boccioni: *Development of a Bottle in Space*, silver plated bronze, 1912.

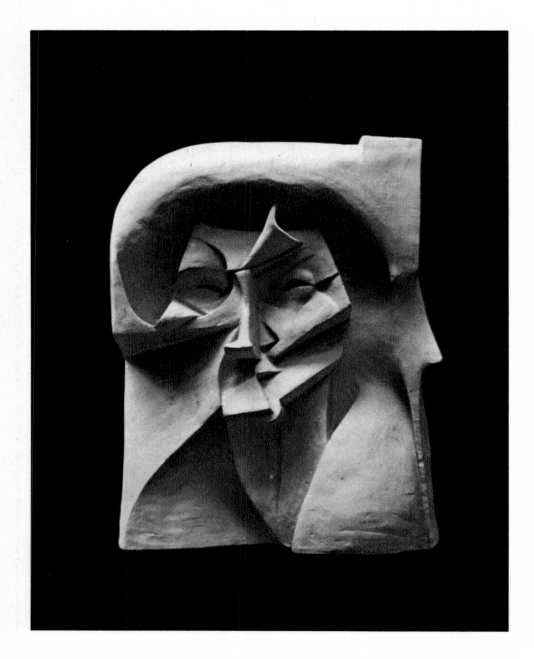

Pl. III - Umberto Boccioni: *Empty and Full Abstracts of a Head*, bronze, 1913.

Pl. IV - Umberto Boccioni: *Portrait of His Mother (Antigrazioso)*, bronze, 1913.

Pl. V - Umberto Boccioni: *Synthesis of Human Dynamism*, plaster, 1912.

Pl. VI - Umberto Boccioni: *Unique Forms in the Continuity of Space*, bronze, 1913.

Pl. VII - Amedeo Modigliani (1884-1920): *Caryatid*, stone, 1915 (?).

Pl. VIII - Amedeo Modigliani: *Head*, stone, 1913 (?).

Pl. IX - Arturo Martini (1889-1947): *Clair de Lune*, terracotta, 1932.

Pl. X - Arturo Martini: *Motherhood* (detail), wood, 1927.

Pl. XI - Arturo Martini: *Woman Swimming Underwater*, marble, 1941.

Pl. XII - Arturo Martini: *Daedalus and Icarus*.

Pl. XIII - Arturo Martini: *Livy*, marble, 1939.

Pl. XIV - Arturo Martini: *Rape of the Sabine Women*, bronze, 1940.

Pl. XV - Arturo Martini: *The Partisan Masaccio*, marble, 1946.

Pl. XVI - Arturo Martini: *Heroic Group*, bronze, study, 1935.

Pl. XVII - Francesco Messina (1900): *Bianca*, polychrome terracotta, 1938.

Pl. XVIII - Francesco Messina: *Beatrice*, bronze, 1959.

Pl. XIX - Giacomo Manzù (1908): *Grand Pas de Danse*, bronze, 1955-59.

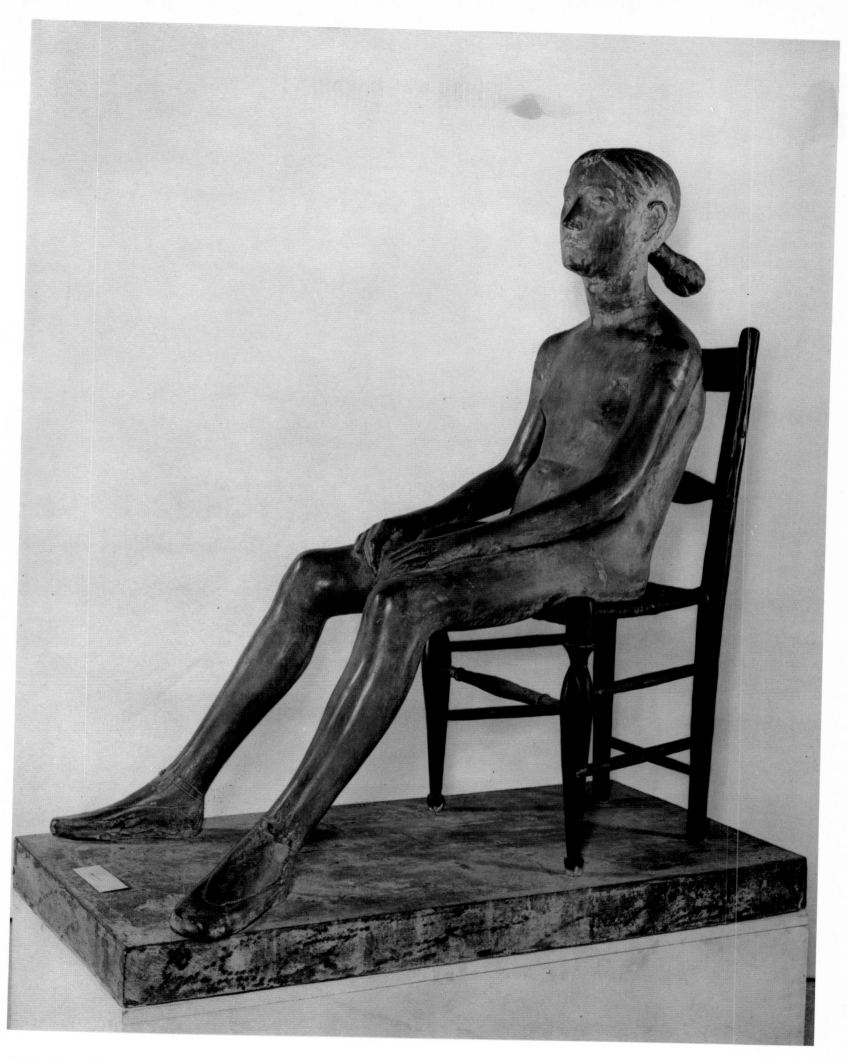

Pl. XX - Giacomo Manzù: *Girl on a Chair*, bronze, 1949.

Pl. XXI - Giacomo Manzù: *Bust of Inge*, bronze, 1960.

Pl. XXII - Giacomo Manzù: *Portrait*, bronze.

Pl. XXIII - Giacomo Manzù: *Cardinal*, bronze 1958.

Pl. XXIV - Giacomo Manzù: *Cardinal*, bronze, 1950.

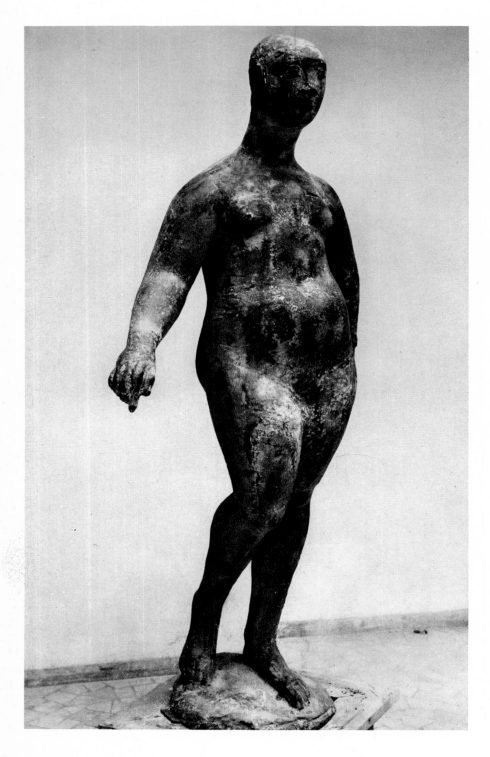

Pl. XXV - Marino Marini (1901): *Pomona*, bronze, 1949.

Pl. XXVI - Marino Marini: *Young Girl*, bronze, 1943.

Pl. XXVII - Marino Marini: *Horse and Rider*, bronze, 1952-53.

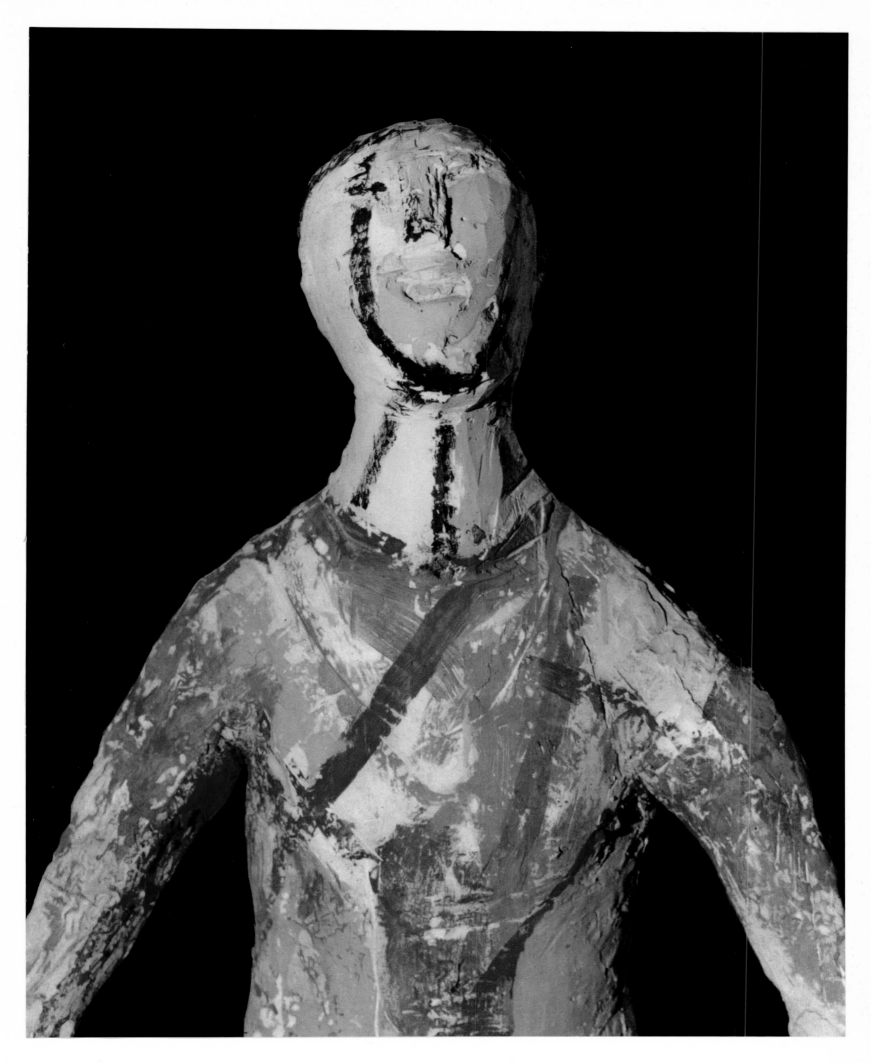

Pl. XXVIII - Marino Marini: *Juggler*, polychrome plaster, 1955.

Pl. XXIX - Marino Marini: *The Miracle*, stone, 1953-54.

Pl. XXX - Marino Marini: *Little Horseman*, polychrome plaster, 1953.

Pl. XXXI - Marcello Mascherini (1906): *Faun*, bronze, 1958.

Pl. XXXII - Marcello Mascherini: *Sappho* (detail), bronze, 1958.

Pl. XXXIII - Marcello Mascherini: *Corrida*, bronze, 1960.

Pl. XXXIV - Marcello Mascherini: *Chimera* (detail), bronze, 1960.

Pl. XXXV - Emilio Greco (1913): *Large Bather No. 1*, (detail), bronze, 1956.

Pl. XXXVI - Emilio Greco: *Crouching Figure,* terracotta, 1956.

Pl. XXXVII - Emilio Greco: *Monument to Pinocchio* (detail), bronze, 1956.

Pl. XXXVIII - Emilio Greco: *Portrait of a woman*, bronze.

Pl. XXXIX - Adriano Alloati (1909): *Study No. 13 for the Large Naiad No. 17*, bronze.

Pl. XL - Adriano Alloati: *Naiad No. 17,* bronze.

Pl. XLI - Dante Zamboni (1905): *Rape of the Nymph*, bronze, 1961.

Pl. XLII - Dante Zamboni: *Dancer*, bronze, 1959.

Pl. XLIII - Pericle Fazzini (1913): *Seated Girl*, plaster, 1954.

Pl. XLIV - Pericle Fazzini: *Sibyl*, bronze, 1947.

Pl. XLV - Pericle Fazzini: *Squatting Woman.*

Pl. XLVI - Pericle Fazzini: *Acrobats*, bronze, 1948.

Pl. XLVII - Marino Mazzacurati (1908): *Monument to the Resistance*, Parma, bronze, 1955.

Pl. XLVIII - Marino Mazzacurati: *Monument to the Resistance* (detail), 1955.

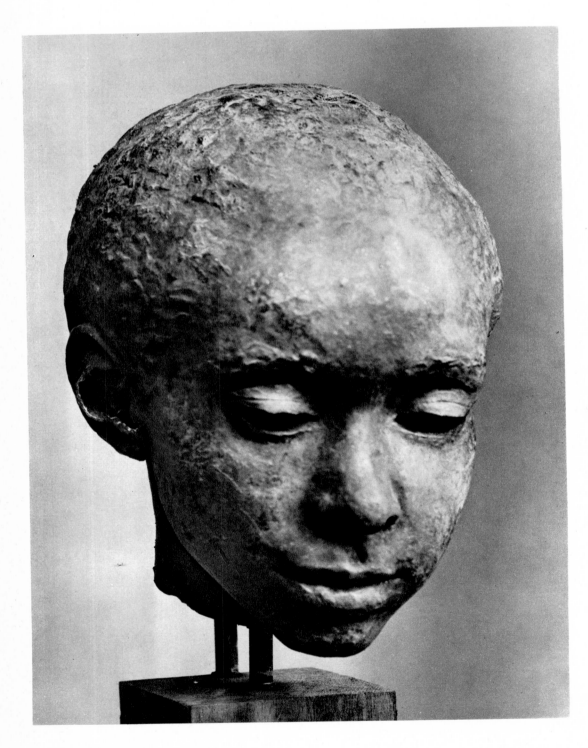

Pl. XLIX - Oscar Gallo (1909): *Small Head*, wax, 1957.

Pl. L - Oscar Gallo: *Portrait*, terracotta, 1958.

Pl. LI - Luigi Broggini (1908): *Victory with Clipped Wings*, bronze, 1959.

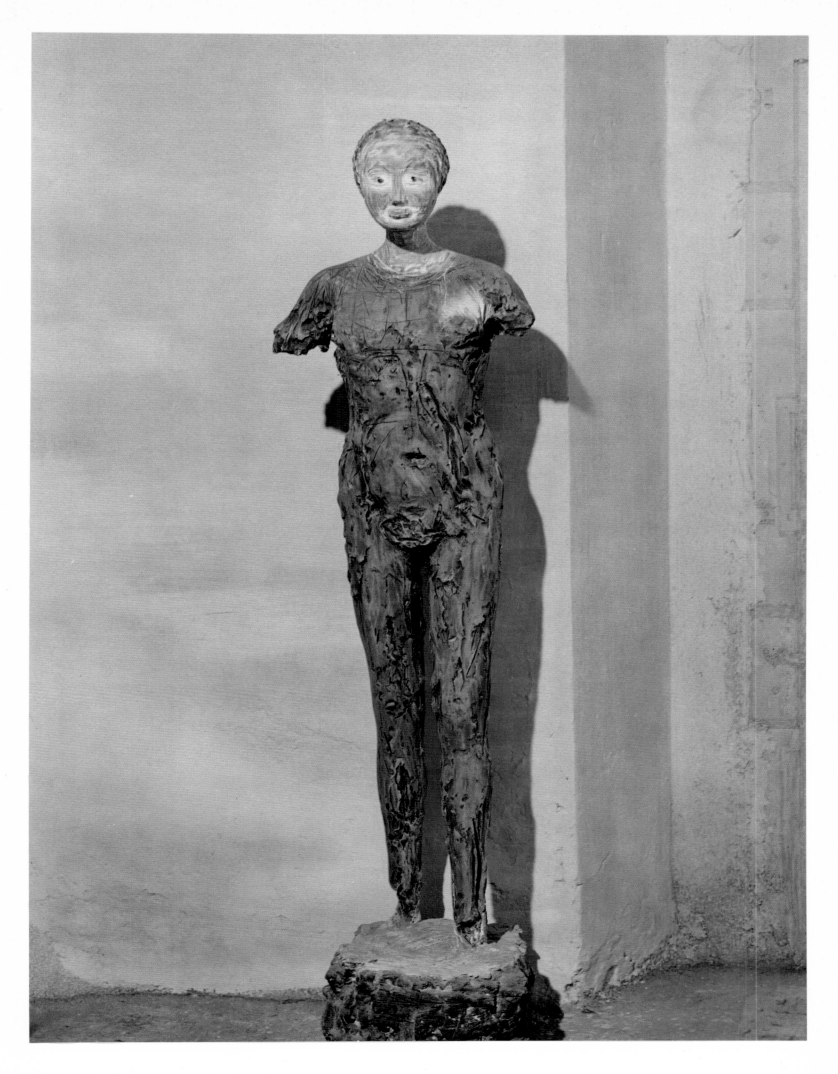

Pl. LII - Luigi Broggini: *Figure,* polychrome terracotta, 1959.

Pl. LIII - Leoncillo (Leonardi) (1915): *White Cut*, ceramic, 1959.

Pl. LIV - Leoncillo (Leonardi): *Black Cut*, ceramic, 1959.

Pl. LV - Luciano Minguzzi (1911): *Two Shadows*, bronze, 1957.

Pl. LVI - Luciano Minguzzi: *Two Forms*, plaster.

Pl. LVII - Luciano Minguzzi: *Shadows in the Wood*, bronze, 1956.

Pl. LVIII - Luciano Minguzzi: *Prisoner in the Lager*.

Pl. LIX - Mirko (Basaldella) (1910): *Warrior Dance*, bronze, 1958.

Pl. LX - Mirko (Basaldella): *Mausoleum of the Fosse Ardeatine* (detail), bronze, 1950.

Pl. LXI - Mirko (Basaldella): *Warrior*, bronze, 1958.

Pl. LXII - Mirko (Basaldella): *Figure*, colored iron, 1960.

Pl. LXIII - Agenore Fabbri (1911): *Big Bird*, Bronze, 1956.

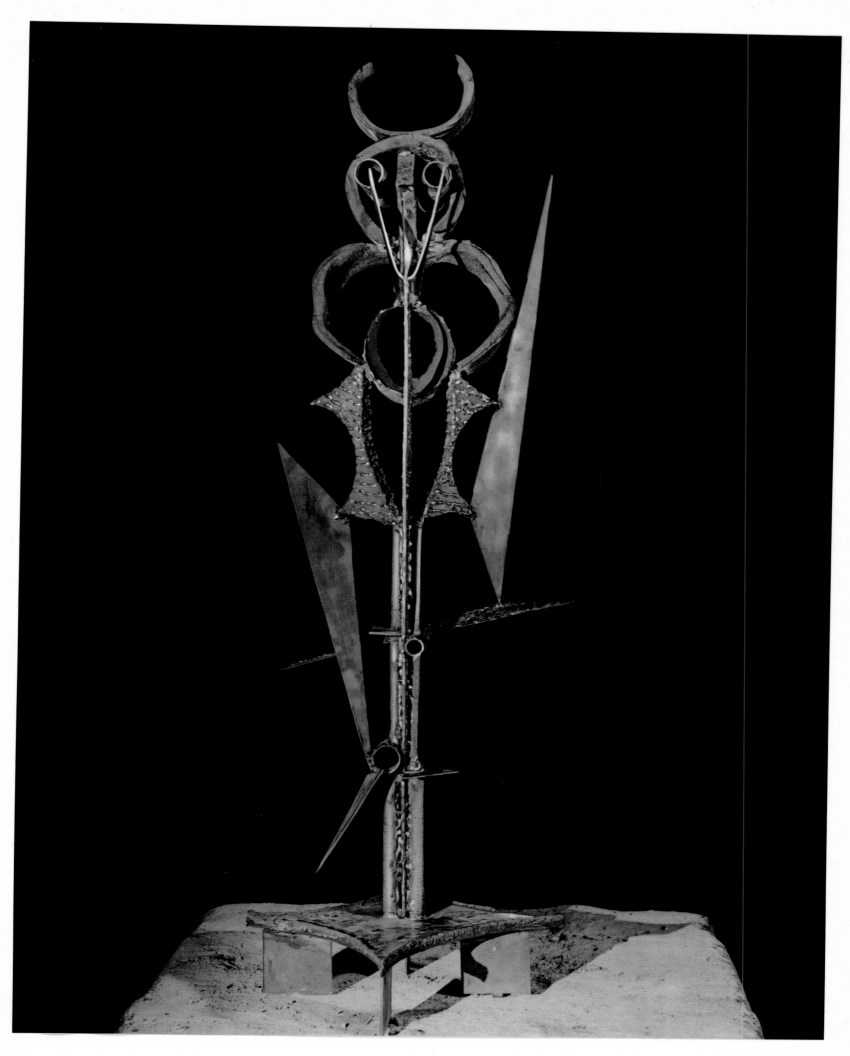

Pl. LXIV - Agenore Fabbri: *Night Bird*, bronze.

Pl. LXV - Raffaello Salimbeni (1916): *Space Man*, bronze, 1960.

Pl. LXVI - Raffaello Salimbeni: *Anna with a Fan*, bronze, 1961.

Pl. LXVII - Chió (Ernesto Galeffi) (1917): *Fish*, bronze, 1960.

Pl. LXVIII - Chió (Ernesto Galeffi): *Bird*, bronze, 1959.

Pl. LXIX - Lucio Fontana (1899): *Spatial Concept, "Nature"*, Sandstone, 1960.

Pl. LXX - Lucio Fontana: *Spatial Concept, "Expectation"*, colored cloth, 1959.

Pl. LXXI - Umberto Mastroianni (1910): *Cavalcade*, bronze, 1959.

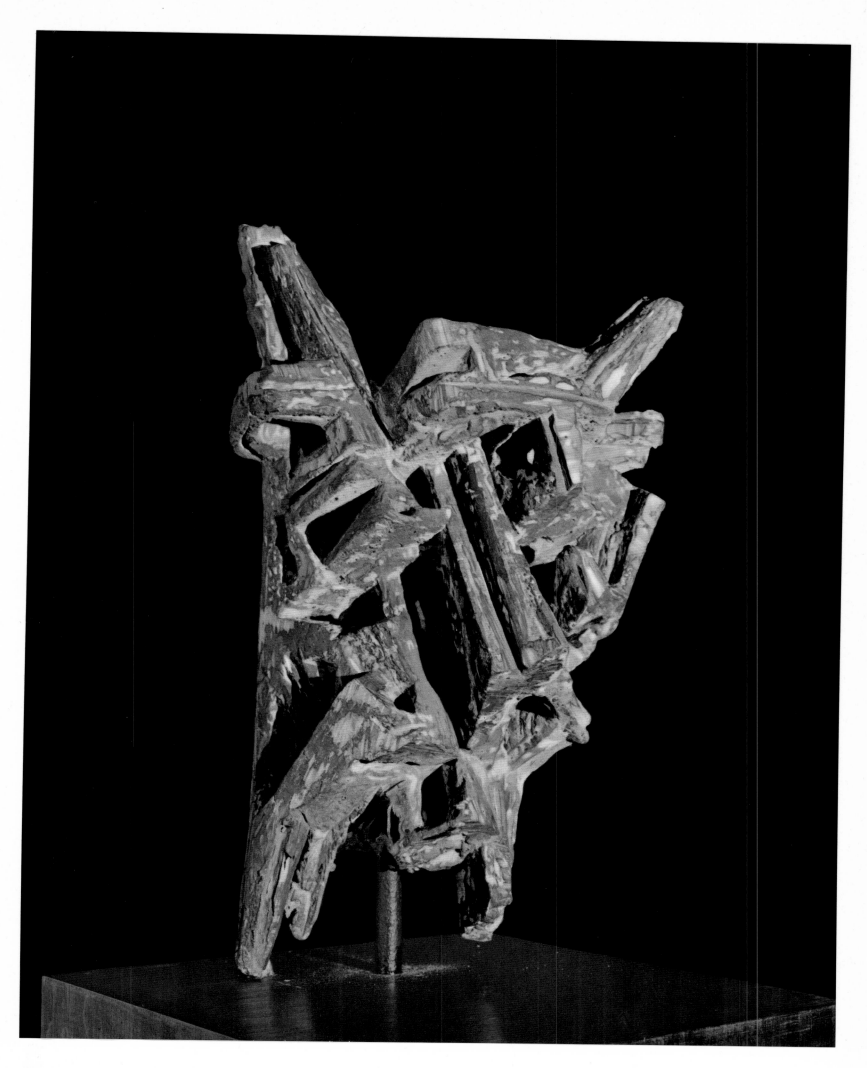

Pl. LXXII - Umberto Mastroianni: *Solomon*, bronze, 1959.

Pl. LXXIII - Francesco Somaini (1926): *Large Bleeding Martyrdom*, bronze, 1960.

Pl. LXXIV - Francesco Somaini: *Vertical (Absalom)*, iron, 1960.

Pl. LXXV - Pietro Consagra (1920): *Oracle of the Chelsea Hotel*, bronze, 1960.

Pl. LXXVI - Pietro Consagra: *Dialogue at S. Angelo*, bronze, 1960.

Pl. LXXVII - Berto Lardera (1911): *Sculpture No. 1*, iron, 1953.

Pl. LXXVIII - Berto Lardera: *Ancient Deity No. 3*, stainless steel and iron, 1958.

Pl. LXXIX - Umberto Milani (1912): *Hermetic Vision*, stone, 1953.

Pl. LXXX - Umberto Milani: *Mode*, bronze, 1959.

Pl. LXXXI - Carmelo Cappello (1912): *Lunar Caprice*, iron, 1959.

Pl. LXXXII - Carmelo Cappello: *Water Skis*, bronze, 1957.

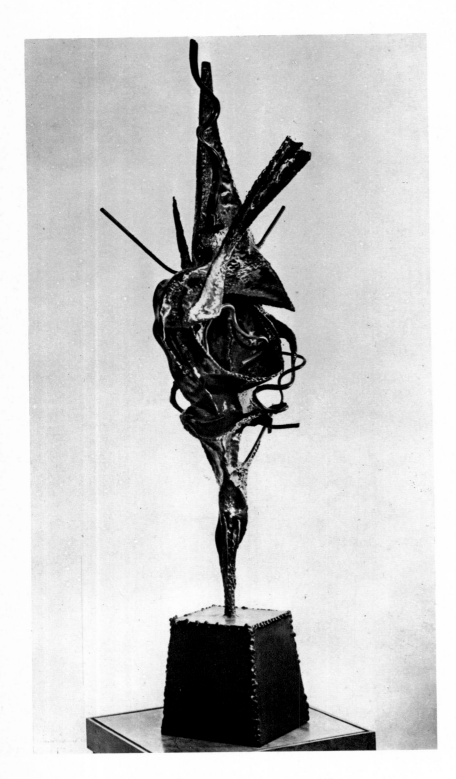

Pl. LXXXIII - Nino Franchina (1912): *Ettore Fieramosca*, iron, 1960.

Pl. LXXXIV - Nino Franchina: *L'oiseau de feu,* iron, 1960.

Pl. LXXXV - Aldo Calò (1910): *Biform*, bronze and crystal, 1960.

Pl. LXXXVI - Aldo Calò: *Nude*, wood, 1943.

Pl. LXXXVII - Alberto Viani (1906): *Sculpture*, plaster, 1958.

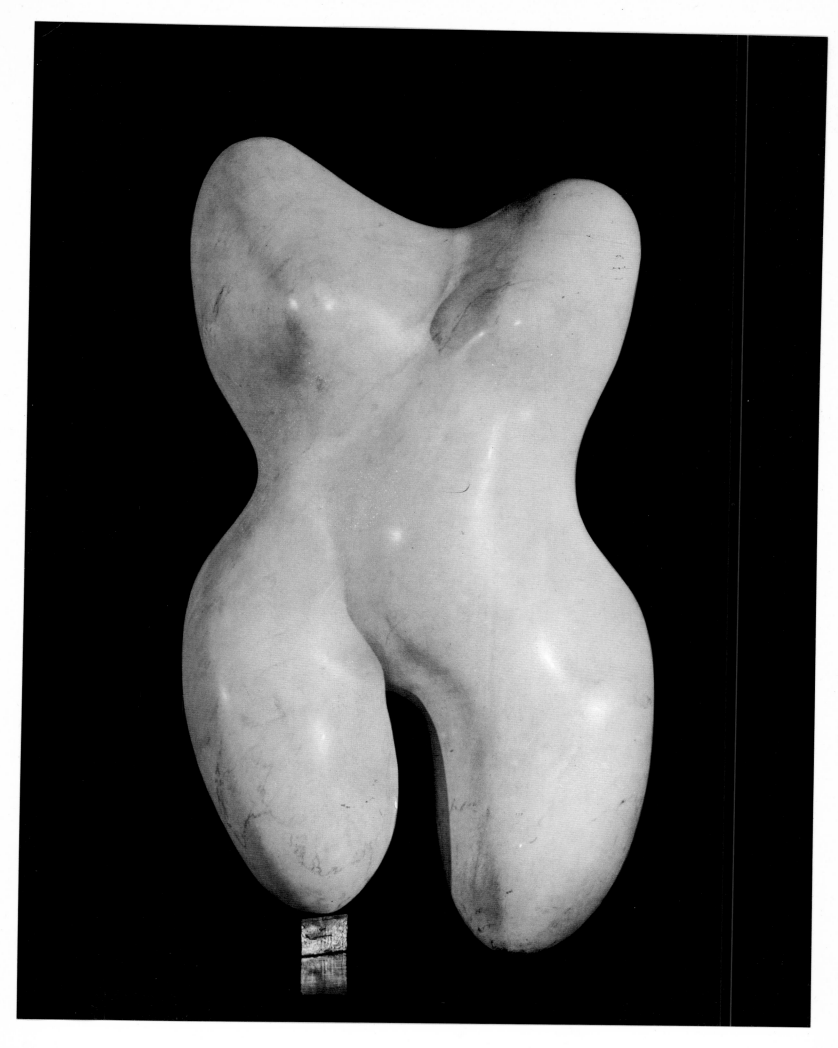

Pl. LXXXVIII - Alberto Viani: *Female Torso*, marble, 1945.

Pl. LXXXIX - Alberto Viani: *Sculpture*, plaster, 1960

Pl. XC - Alberto Viani: *Female Torso*, marble, 1954.

Pl. XCI - Gio Pomodoro (1930): *Study for the Crowd*, plaster, 1957.

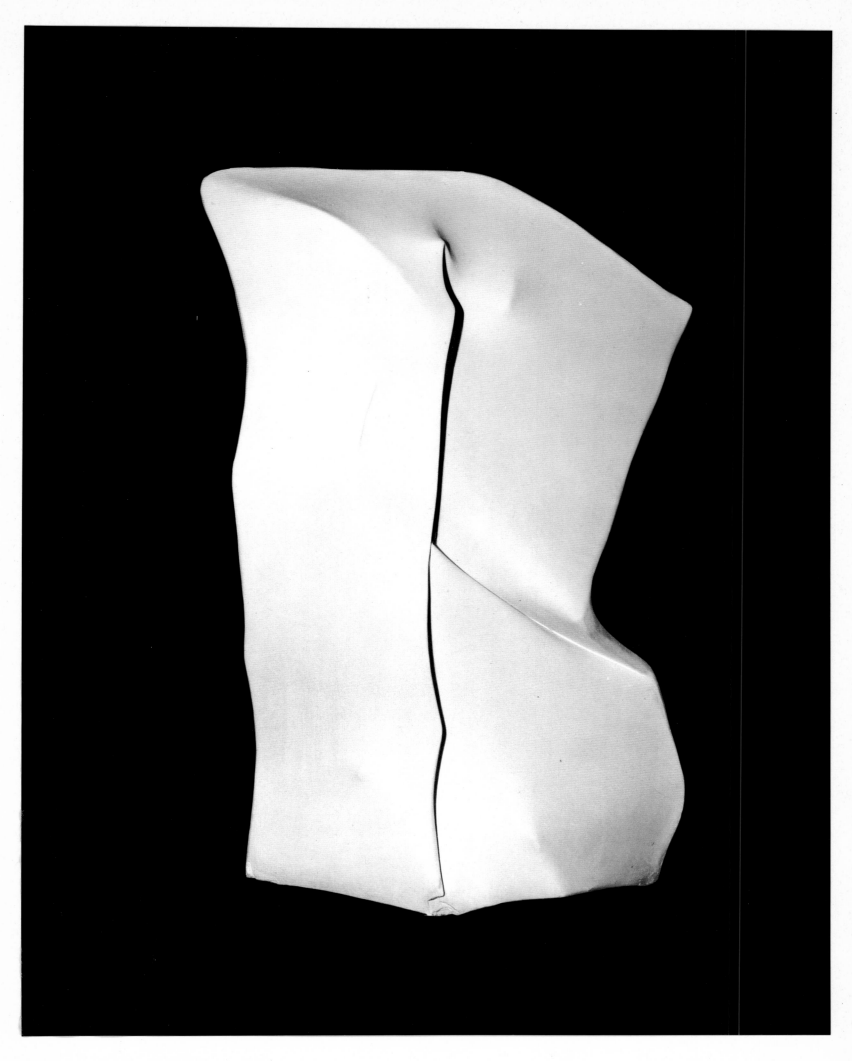

Pl. XCII - Gio Pomodoro: *Co-existence*, plaster, 1960.

Pl. XCIII - Augusto Perez (1929): *Great Queen* (detail), black concrete, 1959.

Pl. XCIV - Augusto Perez: *King and Queen*, bronze, 1959.

LIST OF ILLUSTRATIONS

Note: The illustrations in the text have Arabic numerals; all others Roman numerals. An asterisk (*) preceding the number indicates a colorplate.